D1155367

Bantam Books by Eric W. Johnson
Ask your bookseller for the books you have missed

LOVE AND SEX IN PLAIN LANGUAGE
SEX: TELLING IT STRAIGHT
V. D.

LOVE AND SEX IN PLAIN LANGUAGE
NEW REVISED EDITION
BY ERIC W. JOHNSON
GERMANTOWN FRIENDS SCHOOL

Illustrations by Russ Hoover
Foreword by Emily H. Mudd, Ph.D.

BANTAM BOOKS
TORONTO NEW YORK LONDON

For a Teacher's Guide to this book write to:

Bantam Books, Inc.
S & C Dept.
666 Fifth Avenue
New York, N. Y. 10019

RLI: $\dfrac{\text{VLM 7 (VLR 6-9)}}{\text{IL 8+}}$

LOVE AND SEX IN PLAIN LANGUAGE
*A Bantam Book / published by arrangement with
J. B. Lippincott Company*

PRINTING HISTORY
Lippincott edition published May 1965
2nd printing ...... May 1965   4th printing .... January 1966
3rd printing ...... June 1965   5th printing ...... May 1966
*Lippincott Revised edition published February 1967
2nd printing..November 1967*
New revised Lippincott edition published December 1973

*Bantam Pathfinder edition / May 1968
Seven printings through June 1973*

*Revised Bantam Pathfinder edition / August 1974
2nd printing......January 1975
Bantam edition / August 1976*

Illustration on page 38, "Birth of baby," from The Individual,
Sex, and Society, *edited by Carlfred Broderick and Jessie
Bernard, 1969. Reprinted by permission of The Johns Hopkins
University Press.*

ISBN: 0-553-10039-4

Published simultaneously in the United States and Canada

Contents

Foreword

In the area of love and sex, the old adage "What you don't know won't hurt you" doesn't work. What you don't know may very well hurt you—and those around you. This book, *Love and Sex in Plain Language,* tells eleven- to fifteen-year-olds—and their parents— things they need to know to help avoid hurt and, even more important, to build a sensible and constructive value system on the basis of which they may experience pleasure and good human communication.

I agree with Dr. Joseph Stokes, former president of the American Pediatric Association, that the facts and issues concerning love, sex, the origins of life, and human sexual behavior are presented in this book with "charm and candor," and that they will help the strongly and rightly curious young to engage in healthy give-and-take discussion with their parents and teachers.

The period of early adolescence is a time for emphasizing prevention instead of cure. A valuable means for developing responsible decision-making, for preventing trouble, and for laying the groundwork for the healthy enjoyment of sexuality is to provide, as Eric Johnson does, knowledge of anatomy, of sexual physiology, of intimacies, and of methods for avoiding disease and unwanted pregnancy. With information such as this, presented frankly and understandably, ignorance can no longer serve as an excuse for behavior that may result in disaster or for fears that may take much of the joy out of living and loving.

In my professional life, I have spent many hours with young people and parents discussing their feelings and attitudes about the loving side of life and helping them to communicate about their behavior and relationships. I have long since learned how different from one another people are and how vital it is to understand and respect their differences, which are based both on the genes with which each one begins life and the environment within which each develops. I believe that this book respects these differences, and especially the differences in conviction that its readers will bring to it. I think it can help the growth of a new potential of strength, happiness, and responsible action for young and old who read and discuss the clear and practical knowledge it presents.

EMILY H. MUDD, Ph.D.
Professor Emeritus of Family Study in Psychiatry and Consultant in Behavioral Studies, Department of Obstetrics and Gynecology, University of Pennsylvania School of Medicine
Past President of the American Association of Marriage and Family Counselors

Preface
To Parents and Teachers

This book is written for boys and girls of any age. The prose is easy enough for a bright ten-year-old to understand; the information and ideas presented will be useful to many college students. I suggest, when boys and girls show interest in the subject of sex, you let them have the book, but not push it on them. And first read it yourself. Then you will have a common basis for discussion.

The book is based on some common assumptions. I assume that sex is a part of life—only a part, but a healthy and natural part. I assume that the power of sex for good and for evil, for pleasure and for hurt, is so great that we must make every effort to see that it is used responsibly. I assume that to act responsibly people need all the relevant knowledge that they can understand. Mistakes are made, not because of too much knowledge, but because of too little.

But the facts can be understood best in a framework of values; caring, responsibility, self-control, the family, faithfulness, love, respect of self and others, and the goodness of life. I hope this book strengthens these values.

Most sex books for boys and girls do not have an index, I suppose because the writers fear that the readers will turn to the hottest spots and then read no further. This book has a complete index, and I would consider it entirely natural if readers turn first to the topics that interest them most. If they find that these topics are treated frankly, fully, but concisely, then perhaps they will read the book all the way through. But no one should be forced to read more than he or she wants to read.

Also, if people read the entire book, it should be easy for them to find again quickly those parts they need to reread. Few people will be able to absorb all there is in the book during only one reading.

The book is plain, open, and frank. I hope that reading it will make your children and your students more ready to ask questions of you. If they do, I suggest that you answer them as plainly, openly, and frankly as you can. If they do not, don't be too disappointed. A free family dialogue on sexual matters is rare. Most boys and girls, especially after they reach adolescence, just don't seem to want it or, if they want it, to be able to put themselves in a situation to have it.

When my secretary, the mother of three grown children, returned the typed manuscript of the book to me, she had attached this note: "Every family should have a copy of this book *if* they are ready for honesty and are without false modesty." I believe many families, and almost all boys and girls, are ready.

1965   ERIC W. JOHNSON

Preface to the New Revised Edition

I wrote the first edition of this book in 1965. The junior high school boy I quoted, and still quote, on page 17 is now a graduate scholar at Cambridge, England. Much has changed since he was in seventh grade. The "everything" he wanted to know then and his successors want to know now has expanded as the experience, the sexual expectations, and the need for information of young people have expanded.

I still have no illusions that reading a book on sex can turn a selfish, exploitative person into an unselfish, caring one. But experience has shown me that such a book does help to make people more responsible and does help them to form their values and to understand what is involved in trying to live by them.

1973   E. W. J.

Acknowledgments

As can be seen from the list below, I have been unusually fortunate in this new edition, as in the first edition, to have the facts checked and points of view critically analyzed by some of the country's outstanding doctors and specialists in obstetrics and gynecology, psychology, psychiatry, sex education, family planning, and family relations. I am most grateful to them for the many hours of assistance they have given.

Knowledgeable as they all are, they did not always all agree on every point, and the final decisions as to what to say have had to be mine. To all of the following goes the credit for many of the strengths of this book and no blame for any of its shortcomings.

Louise Bates Ames, Ph.D., New Haven; co-founder and co-director, Gesell institute of Child Development.

Derek L. Burleson, Ed.D., New York; Director of Educational and Research Services, Sex Information and Education Council of the United States (SIECUS).

Mary S. Calderone, M.D., M.P.H., New York; Executive Director, Sex Information and Education Council of the United States (SIECUS); former Medical Director, Planned Parenthood Federation of America.

Warren J. Gadpaille, M.D., Englewood, Colorado; Psychoanalyst; Committee on Adolescence of the Group for the Advancement of Psychiatry; Consultant in Family Living for Jefferson County School District, Colorado; Vice-President, American Association of Sex Educators and Counselors, Washington, D.C.

Alan F. Guttmacher, M.D., New York; Emeritus Clinical Professor of Obstetrics and Gynecology, College of Physicians and Surgeons, Columbia University; President, Planned Parenthood and World Population; author: *Birth Control and Love* (formerly *The Complete Book of Birth Control*); *Understanding Sex, A Young Person's Guide; Pregnancy, Birth and Family Planning*.

Marjorie W. Hackmann, Corvallis, Oregon; feminist; author: *Practical Sex Information*.

W. Meredith Heyl, M.D., Philadelphia; Obstetrician and Gynecologist to the Germantown and Chestnut Hill Hospitals; Assistant Professor of Obstetrics and Gynecology, School of Medicine, Temple University.

Corinne B. Johnson, Philadelphia; Director, Latin American Program, International Service Division, American Friends Service Committee (Quakers); co-author: *Love and Sex and Growing Up*.

Winifred Kempton, Philadelphia; Education Director, Planned Parenthood Association of Southeastern Pennsylvania; author: *Techniques for Leading Group Discussions on Human Sexuality*.

Lester A. Kirkendall, Ph.D., Portland, Oregon; Professor of Family Life, formerly Oregon State University; author: *Premarital Intercourse and Interpersonal Relations*.

Genevieve Millet Landau, New York; Editor-in-Chief, *Parents' Magazine*.

Paul Lecky, Jr., M.D., Philadelphia; Staff Psychiatrist, Philadelphia Child Guidance Clinic.

Harold I. Lief, M.D., Philadelphia; Director, Division of Family Study, Department of Psychiatry, School of Medicine, University of Pennsylvania.

Janice Lindsay, Philadelphia; teacher of science, Germantown Friends School, Philadelphia.

Luigi Mastroianni, Jr., M.D., Philadelphia; William Goodell Professor and Department Chairman of Obstetrics and Gynecology, University of Pennsylvania School of Medicine.

John Money, Ph.D., Baltimore; Professor of Medical Psychology and Associate Professor of Pediatrics, Johns Hopkins University School of Medicine and Hospital; President, 1974–76, Society for the Scientific Study of Sex; author: *Sex Errors of the Body;* co-author: *Man and Woman, Boy and Girl: The Differentiation and Dimorphism of Gender Identity from Conception to Maturity.*

Emily H. Mudd, Ph.D., Philadelphia; Professor Emeritus of Family Study in Psychiatry, School of Medicine, University of Pennsylvania; Associate Director, Continuing Education, Reproductive Biology Research Foundation, St. Louis; Consultant, Department of Obstetrics and Gynecology, University of Pennsylvania; author: *Success in Family Living.*

Elaine C. Pierson, M.D., Ph.D., Philadelphia; Office of Gynecology, Student Health Service, University of Pennsylvania; author: *Sex Is Never an Emergency; Female and Male: The Sexual Context.*

Patricia Schiller, M.A., J.D., Washington, D.C.; Executive Director, American Association of Sex Education and Counselors; Assistant Professor, College of Medicine, Howard University.

Walter R. Stokes, LL.B., M.D., Stuart, Florida; retired psychiatrist and sex educator; author: *Married Love in Today,s World; Modern Pattern for Marriage;* co-author: *45 Levels to Sexual Understanding and Enjoyment.*

E.W.J.

1

Why Talk Plainly
About Love and Sex?

After school one day I gave a lift home to a junior high school boy I was teaching. He had read a book I had written about junior high school, and he asked, "Mr. Johnson, are you ever going to write another book?"

I told him I planned to write one about sex and that it would be primarily for boys and girls his age. "I'm having a hard time deciding how much to put into it," I told him. "Perhaps you can help me. What do you think people your age want to know about sex?"

"Everything!" he replied at once and with a sure smile.

And every junior-high-schooler I have talked with since then has given almost the same reply: **everything.** So I decided that in this book I would try to tell everything, and to tell it in plain language.

But before we get down to the detailed facts of sex and love, I want you to understand a few general ideas, which will help you to understand the facts better.

Everyone of almost any age is interested in sex, in the difference between boys and girls and men and women, in lovemaking, in what starts babies, and in how they develop and are born. They are interested in questions about sexual behavior and feelings, about sex outside of the family as well as inside. Your own interest in these things, even though you may find it difficult to admit it to everyone or even to yourself, is perfectly normal. After all, why shouldn't a person want to know all about such an important and universal a thing as sex? Without it the human race would soon disappear. Also, it effects our most important human relationships and can be one of our greatest pleasures.

Many parents and other grownups are uncomfortable when they try to talk with boys and girls about sex. Perhaps your parents have talked with you about it; perhaps they have not. Perhaps, like many adults, they have been brought up to believe that sex is very personal and private. Thus, it is easy to understand why they may hesitate to discuss it with you.

A young girl wrote to me once saying that it was difficult for her to get any information about sex from her parents because she was too embarrassed to start asking questions. She told me that when she finally did get the courage to ask one, her father said, "See your mother," and her mother said, "I'm busy."

Perhaps after you have read this book you will be able to ask questions and express opinions more easily, and that will make it easier for your parents to try to answer and to listen to your opinions and give you theirs.

Because people's interest in sex is so natural and so strong, yet because people so often don't want to talk about it, many wrong ideas get passed around. You can help others as well as yourself by learning the facts and by correcting any wrong ideas you may hear. If you have questions that aren't answered, the only intelligent thing to do is to ask them of a mature person you respect and who knows the answers, preferably your mother or father, your teacher, clergyman, or doctor. And, of course, there are lots of questions about sexual behavior that you will keep trying to answer all your life.

Many boys and girls don't like to admit there's anything about sex that they don't know. Surely the best policy is to admit you don't know and to find out. Most people will respect you for this.

Sex is a powerful urge. By the time people reach their middle teens, their interest in and desire for sexual activity may be very strong. However, the strength of the sex urge varies from person to person and from time to time, and in many people other interests are stronger.

The important thing for you to know is that sex can be a wonderful expression of love between people and can give great pleasure. But it can also cause much suffering if used selfishly or ignorantly. It can create families and bind them together; it can damage and disrupt them. Later chapters will say more about these matters.

2

The Woman's Sex Organs and How They Develop and Work

Now let's turn to specific facts about sex. In this chapter I'll tell you about girls and women, and, in the one that follows, about boys and men.

You may have seen something of the sex life of domestic animals; you know where kittens and puppies come from and, even if you live in the city, where calves and lambs come from. You know that a dog is either a male or a female and that it is easy to tell which, and that the same applies to people.

Here now are the details about the sexual system of the woman. As I explain it to you, refer to the drawings of a grown woman on the following page and to the more detailed diagram of her **genitals**—sexual parts.

The **ovaries** are where the egg cells (**ova**) are stored. These two organs are inside the lower part of the abdomen, one on either side, and are the shape of a flattened oval and about 1¼ to 2½ inches long. When a girl baby is born, her ovaries already contain, in undeveloped form, tens of thousands of egg cells. Four to five hundred of them will mature during her lifetime. But the ovaries are inactive until a girl reaches **puberty.** Then, around the ages of eleven to fourteen, they begin a monthly process which is repeated more or less regularly until a woman reaches the age of forty-five (or possibly younger) to fifty-five. During these thirty to forty years, every twenty-one to thirty-five days, a mature egg (**ovum**) is

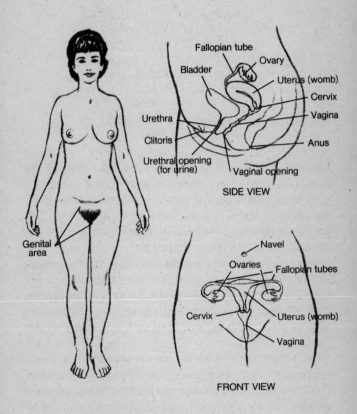

Fallopian tube
Ovary
Bladder
Uterus (womb)
Cervix
Urethra
Vagina
Clitoris
Anus
Urethral opening
(for urine)
Vaginal opening
Genital
area
SIDE VIEW

Navel
Ovaries
Fallopian tubes
Cervix
Uterus (womb)
Vagina
FRONT VIEW

produced by one or the other ovary. (The ovaries do not necessarily alternate the task.) The egg cell is very small. A row of two hundred would be only about an inch long. The ovum bursts through the surface of the ovary and enters the **fallopian tube** just next to it, helped by the tube's fingerlike fringes, called **fimbria**. This process is called **ovulation,** and occasionally some women can feel

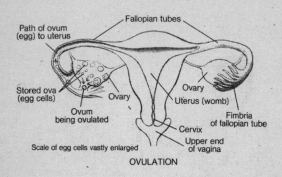

Path of ovum (egg) to uterus
Fallopian tubes
Stored ova (egg cells)
Ovary
Ovum being ovulated
Ovary
Uterus (womb)
Fimbria of fallopian tube
Cervix
Scale of egg cells vastly enlarged
Upper end of vagina

OVULATION

a twinge in the lower abdomen within a day or so of the time it happens, but not always just when it happens.

After ovulation, the ovum is moved slowly down the fallopian tube toward the **uterus** (also called the **womb,** pronounced "woom"). This organ, located between the ovaries, is pear-shaped and about 3 inches long in a mature female who has not had children. It is muscular and elastic and can grow and stretch to many times this size. The uterus is the organ in which a baby grows until it is ready to be born, and whose powerful muscles help to push the baby out through the **vagina** into the world.

Every month or so the uterus prepares for a fertilized egg, an egg which may grow into a baby. It creates a nourishing soft webbing, or velvety lining, of tiny, delicate blood vessels—a perfect place for the egg to grow in. If an egg is fertilized, it has already started to grow by the time it enters the uterus, about three or four days after it left the ovary.

However, if an egg is not fertilized, it stays alive for

only about twelve to twenty-four hours after entering the fallopian tube, and then it breaks up and is absorbed into the body. In this case, the growing place in the uterus is

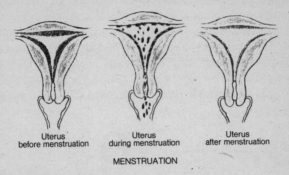

Uterus
before menstruation

Uterus
during menstruation

Uterus
after menstruation

MENSTRUATION

not needed, and the lining, blood, and blood vessels are discarded through the vagina and out of the body. This monthly event is called **menstruation** (when a woman says she is "having her period") and lasts from three to six days. Menstruation is not bleeding in the ordinary sense of the word, although the fluid is red and contains blood, on the average about three tablespoonfuls. Menstruation is mainly the discarding of some blood and tissues that are now of no use.

How can a girl know when she is about to have her first period? **The "timetable" is different for each girl.** In both boys and girls, generally somewhere between the ages of nine and eighteen, there occurs a period of rapid growth that we call a **growth spurt.** It lasts about three years, and during the girl's time of greatest growth, her height increases from 2½ to 4½ inches in a single year. Girls generally, not always, begin their growth spurt about two years before boys. This means that from the ages of a little over eleven until about fourteen girls go through a period when they are, on the average, a bit

taller than boys of the same age. A girl's first menstruation may come at almost any time during her growth
spurt, or sometimes even after it is over. Most often,
however, it comes about three quarters of the way
through, and a year after her year of peak growth.

On the average—and remember, most people aren't
just at the average—about three to four years before a
girl's first menstruation her **breasts** begin to swell. In
most girls, the breasts become noticeable two or three
years before menstruation. A year and a half to two and a

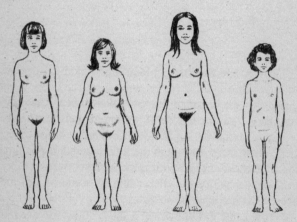

FOUR NORMAL TEEN-AGE GIRLS OF THE SAME AGE

half years before, **pubic hair** appears above her genitals
and, about six months before, other hair appears under
her arms.

A girl's first menstruation is the sign that she has
reached puberty, that she is becoming capable of her part
in producing a child. However, in many girls there is a gap
of several months to a year or more between the first
menstruation and the first ovulation. In other words, the

first menstruation does not necessarily mean that a girl is immediately capable of having a baby. On the other hand, it is possible for a young girl to become pregnant even **before** her first menstruation; that is, a few girls may ovulate for the first time before they ever menstruate.

Generally, the first menstruation occurs between the ages of eleven and fourteen. However, some girls menstruate as early as nine, and a few not until they are fifteen, sixteen, or seventeen. **No girl need worry because she arrives at any part of the timetable sooner or later than her friends;** she is almost certain to be ahead of some and behind others. If she is worried, it is a simple matter for her to be examined by a **gynecologist**—a doctor who specializes in the health problems of women—for assurance that her development is normal, and for any needed treatment if it is not.

When a girl begins to menstruate, it means that her body is now maturing, but not for several years will she be mature enough to undertake the responsibilities of marriage and childbearing. Menstruation marks the beginning of **adolescence** for a girl. Adolescence is the period of perhaps eight years during which a girl is neither a child nor an adult, but a **person** on the way to becoming an adult.

Menstruation can be inconvenient. Some women,

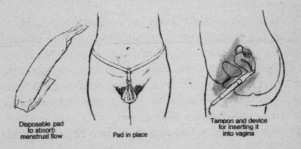

Disposable pad
to absorb
menstrual flow

Pad in place

Tampon and device
for inserting it
into vagina

half humorously, even call it "the curse." When menstruation starts, many girls use a disposable **pad** or **napkin** to absorb the menstrual flow. It is made of cellulose or other absorbent material in a gauze covering and comes in two or three sizes. It can be held in place along the opening of the vagina by an elastic panty, a belt or a sticky backing that clings to the panty. Many girls use a different menstrual aid called a **tampon** or **insert.** Tampons also come in different sizes. They are made of absorbent material shaped into a small roll for easy insertion into the vagina, where they absorb the flow.

DIFFERENT TYPES OF HYMEN
(In some girls and women the hymen may be entirely absent.)

Some girls may not at first be able to use a tampon because the entrance to the vagina is partly closed by a **membrane** called the **hymen.** (A membrane is a thin, sheetlike layer of living tissue.) However, if they start with a small-size tampon and slowly stretch the hymenal opening, most girls soon will be able to use this convenient menstrual aid.

Many people mistakenly believe that it is possible to tell whether or not a girl is a **virgin** (a female who has not had sexual intercourse) by whether her hymen is unbroken or broken. However, this is not a reliable sign, because in many girls an ample opening in the hymen develops quite naturally, or the hymen may even be almost entirely absent at birth.

When a girl is approaching her first **menstrual**

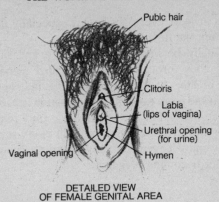

- Pubic hair
- Clitoris
- Labia (lips of vagina)
- Urethral opening (for urine)
- Vaginal opening
- Hymen

DETAILED VIEW
OF FEMALE GENITAL AREA

period, she should talk with her mother and get the needed equipment.

Sometimes girls and women find the few days before and during early menstruation difficult. They may have abdominal pains or aches in the lower back as the muscles of the uterus contract to discard the unneeded lining. They may also have headaches or feel depressed and edgy. Tears or temper may come rather easily. Girls can be comforted by knowing that many women feel the same way, that the feelings will go away in a day or two. Sometimes a girl needs the advice of a doctor to help her have a more comfortable menstrual period.

It may take more than a year for a girl's menstrual periods to become somewhat regular, but this should be no cause for worry. In many women, the periods never become entirely regular, and for almost all women there are occasional times of irregularity.

A girl should lead her normal life during her period. She may participate in school sports. If she swims, she should use a tampon. Cleanliness is important during menstruation, as at all other times, and it is helpful if a girl bathes or showers every day and changes the pad or tampon at least every six hours, especially during the time when the flow is full.

Usually between ages forty-five and fifty-five a woman goes through a process called **menopause** or **change of life.** At the end of this period, her ovaries discharge no more eggs and menstruation ceases. It does not mean the end of her sexual life— only that she can bear no more children. She can still enjoy sex; in fact, she may enjoy it even more now that there is no possibility of her becoming pregnant.

3

The Man's Sex Organs
and How They Develop and Work

Here now are the details about the sex organs of men. These are a remarkable and complicated system of glands, tubes, and containers designed to manufacture the male reproductive cell, called the **sperm,** to store it, and to deliver it into the woman's body.

On the opposite page you see a drawing of a grown man. Next to it are two more detailed drawings of his sexual parts, or genitals. Refer to these diagrams as you read.

A man's most obvious sexual organ is his **penis,** which is usually about the length of a finger, although somewhat larger around. It has a small tube which runs from the bladder down through its center. One purpose of this tube is to empty urine from the bladder. The other purpose, about which I shall say more later, is as a passageway for the sperm.

At birth, the end of a baby boy's penis is usually covered by a sheath of skin called the **foreskin.** It is possible to push this skin back, but often it is removed by the doctor just after the baby's birth. This makes it easier to keep the penis clean. Removing the foreskin is called **circumcision.** On page 15 are drawings of an uncircumcised penis and a circumcised one.

Under the man's penis hangs a sac of loose, crinkly skin called the **scrotum,** which contains the two **testicles,** or **testes.** These oval-shaped glands, each about 1½

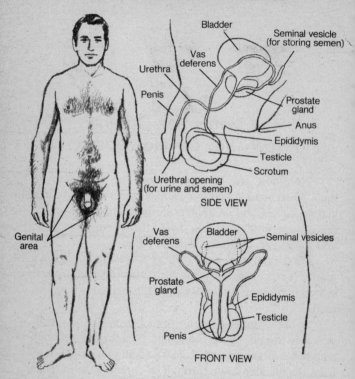

inches long in a grown man, are where the sperm, the male reproductive cells, are made. In most men, one hangs lower than the other. Behind and against each testicle is a storage place, the **epididymis**—really a collection of about half a mile of tiny tubes—where the millions of sperm cells are matured as they pass through. Each sperm cell is shaped like a tadpole with a long, thin tail and is so small that five hundred of them placed end to end would take up only an inch. Sperm can be seen only through a microscope.

From the epididymis the sperm cells travel through a long flexible tube, the **vas deferens** or spermatic duct,

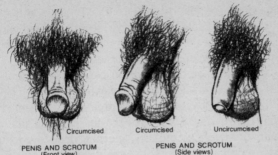

Circumcised   Circumcised   Uncircumcised

PENIS AND SCROTUM
(Front view)

PENIS AND SCROTUM
(Side views)

toward the **seminal vesicles,** which are two small storage pouches at the back of the **prostate gland.** The prostate secretes thick, milky liquid that mixes with the sperm. This mixture is called **semen** and is stored in the seminal vesicles, the prostate, and the upper part of the vas deferens, ready to be discharged through the penis and to start the sperm on its way to the egg cell in the female.

When a man is sexually stimulated, a remarkable change occurs in his penis. This change is called **erection;** it is caused by his body quickly sending a supply of blood into the spongy tissues of the usually limp penis. The penis then grows firm and erect and increases in diameter and in length, becoming commonly from 5 to 8 inches long in a mature man. It stands out from the body at an angle and is then ready for sexual intercourse (see the next chapter). The shape and angle of the erect penis differ with different men.

There is no relation between the size or length of a man's penis and his sexual power, and a penis that is small when limp increases much more during erection than does a penis that is larger when limp. Masters and Johnson, two famous scientists who have studied sexual relations in great detail, have said that "erection is the great equalizer." But the size of the erect penis makes little difference in the sexual pleasure, since a woman's vagina (see p. 5) comfortably stretches to accommodate any size penis, and the **clitoris** (see p. 5) and most sensitive parts of the vagina are near the outside, where even the shortest erect penis can easily reach.

Most teen-age boys and most men have frequent erections, both while awake and while asleep. These may be caused by thoughts or dreams about sex, by reading or listening to music, by the nearness of a girl or a woman, or merely by the early-morning need to urinate. Most erections end without any discharge of semen when the valves in certain veins open and allow the extra supply of blood to return to the main circulation system of the body. When a discharge of semen does occur, it is called an **ejaculation.** It comes as a series of quick, short spurts of milky-white fluid. In most males, after the ejaculation, the penis rather quickly becomes limp again.

In a mature, healthy man each drop of semen contains tens of thousands of **spermatozoa** (sperm cells). Hundreds of millions of spermatozoa are contained in the spoonful or so of semen discharged from the penis during an ejaculation. Yet small as it is, each single

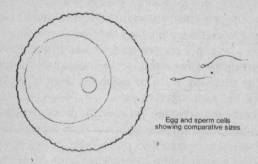

Egg and sperm cells
showing comparative sizes

sperm cell may be capable of uniting with an egg cell inside the female and starting a new human life.

Some people wonder if it is harmful for the semen to travel through the same passage in the penis as that used by the urine, and if semen and urine might get mixed together. There is no such possibility. A special valve in the man's body automatically shuts off the urine while ejaculation is taking place, and the sex glands secrete a special fluid to neutralize any remains of urine before the semen is ejaculated.

How can a boy know when he will begin to produce and ejaculate semen? This event occurs during a boy's adolescent growth spurt, just as the first menstruation does during the growth spurt of a girl. Boys begin and end their growth spurts at very different ages; in fact, some don't begin theirs until others have completed theirs. A boy's rapid increase in height may start anywhere between the ages of ten and sixteen and end between ages thirteen and eighteen. This does not mean that the boy has reached his full height at thirteen to eighteen, only that the period of extra-rapid increase ends somewhere during that period. In a boy's single year of peak growth he may become 2½ to 5 inches taller.

The first ejaculation of semen comes **on the average**—there is great variation from boy to boy—about a year after his penis and testicles have started to grow noticeably, and at about the same time as his year of peak growth. One of the most reliable signs of approaching ejaculation is the appearance, just above the penis, of pubic hair, which is at first downy but which gradually becomes darker and coarser, though not straight. Usually somewhat later, hair also begins to grow under the arms. On the average, three to four months after the first curly pubic hair appears, the first ejaculation with semen comes, although, let me emphasize again, the length of time varies greatly from boy to boy. When a boy first ejaculates semen, we say that he has reached puberty and is entering adolescence.

Often a boy's first ejaculation with semen will occur

at night while he is asleep. He may be having a dream and will awaken to find that semen has been discharged onto his pajamas or the sheet. This is called **nocturnal emission** (it means a nighttime sending out of semen) or "wet dream" and is how the body gets rid of surplus semen. A boy need not feel embarrassed if his mother sees evidence of his emission of semen. She understands perfectly well what has happened and knows that it is a sign that her son's body is now maturing.

Just as often, a boy's first ejaculation will come because he has been **masturbating**—rubbing his penis with his hand or against the bed. Chapter 11 tells more about masturbation.

The change of voice that boys undergo in early adolescence usually begins a few months **after** puberty, although there is great variation in the time. The change is caused by a rather sudden increase in the size of the voice box. This is a part of the young adolescent's spurt of growth.

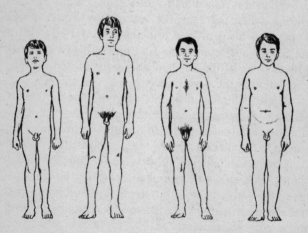

FOUR NORMAL TEEN-AGE BOYS OF THE SAME AGE

It is perfectly normal for a boy to reach puberty as early as age ten or eleven, or perhaps not until he's fifteen or sixteen. As you can see from the drawings of four teen-age boys of the same age, there are great differences at this time of life. Boys need not worry about whether they are ahead of or behind their friends. They will almost certainly be ahead of some and behind others. By the time they are twenty or so, there will be very few important differences in development between them.

The beginning of ejaculation at puberty does not mean that a boy has become a man. It does mean that he has become capable of making a girl pregnant.

4

Man and Woman Unite in Sexual Intercourse

In Chapter 2 you followed the path of the egg cell out of the ovary. In Chapter 3 you read about how the sperm cells were made and discharged from the man's penis. Now let me explain how the sperm leaves the body of the man, enters the body of the woman, and, perhaps, meets the egg.

This process is called mating or **sexual intercourse.** Another work for it is **coitus** [koʹiˑtəs]; and when people speak or write about a man and a woman "going to bed together," "sleeping together," "having sex," "having relations," "making love," or, sometimes, "doing it," they are referring to sexual intercourse. Two very common slang words for intercourse are *fuck* and *screw*. If you look up **intercourse** in a dictionary, you will find that its meaning includes the idea of **exchange** and **communication.** When two people who are deeply in love have intercourse, often they exchange thoughts and feelings; they communicate their love for each other in an intimate and joyous way.

Some couples may have sexual intercourse several times a week, others perhaps only once or twice a month, whatever they feel is right for them. Intercourse and preparation for it may take anywhere from a few minutes to half an hour or more. Different couples may have different styles. The couple might come together and kiss, embrace, and caress each other in all parts of the body. They might speak their love for each other. There are many other ways that they can enjoy this period of **foreplay.** After a time, the woman's mind and body are ready for the act of coitus; her vagina becomes wet with a colorless fluid resulting from sexual excitement. Meanwhile, and usually much more quickly, the man's penis has become erect so that, when the woman is ready, it enters her vagina easily. The man moves his penis in and out inside the vagina, and the woman may also move in various ways. The motions of intercourse cause friction against the concentration of nerve endings in the head of the penis and against similar nerve endings in the very sensitive clitoris (see the diagram on page 5). This stimulation of the penis and clitoris is the main physical cause of **orgasm** in man and in woman, and it gives both great pleasure.

After a time, each partner may reach the climax of sexual pleasure, called an orgasm, a glorious spasm that is impossible to describe adequately in a few words. For the man, orgasm is the moment when the sperm is ejaculated in a series of quick spurts. During intercourse, it takes place inside the vagina close to the neck of the uterus (the **cervix;** see the diagram on page 5). For the woman, the orgasm involves a series of muscular contractions of the walls of the vagina. She has no ejaculation of fluid. For both, the orgasm is accompanied by rapid, heavy breathing and other signs of an exciting climax. A man and woman rather seldom experience orgasm at the same moment. Indeed, some women may rarely or even never experience orgasm. If so, even though they miss a great pleasure, they can still enjoy intercourse. Often, some counseling, probably for both the man and the woman, can help her to achieve orgasm.

After the climax of intercourse, a couple who love and understand each other feel especially close and relaxed. They experience a sense of well-being and contentment together. In other words, although the physical pleasure of intercourse is intense, much more is involved than mere body. It involves a person's feelings, thoughts, and emotions. If intercourse is undertaken outside of a truly loving relationship between man and woman, one based on the caring of each partner for the other, then it can sometimes hurt one or both of the partners and their relationship. Within marriage, intercourse stengthens and intensifies the love that man and wife feel for each other.

Often the first time a couple have intercourse, the event to which they may have been looking forward with expectation of great pleasure is a disappointment. It doesn't turn out to be the ecstasy that each was counting on. For the man, it may all be over too fast; for the woman, it may involve some discomfort, and she very likely will not experience an orgasm, partly because for her, too, it happens too quickly. This can leave her disappointed and frustrated.

Sexual intercourse is something that loving couples **learn to enjoy** more and more as they become more skilled and more aware of each other's feelings. If a man and woman learn how to tell each other, either by words or by signals that each learns to recognize, what feels good, what they like and do not like, then their pleasure in sex together increases. A man can learn to delay his orgasm until his partner becomes more ready for hers; a woman can learn to show her partner how to help her to have a climax. It is especially important for the man to remember that stimulation of the area around the clitoris is very important to most women. It is the experience of many couples that motions of the penis and the thrusting movements of the woman do not provide enough stimulation, and couples will want to discover together other ways of stimulation that they will prefer.

It is important, also, for the couple to feel relaxed

and comfortable and unhurried together. Many couples do not enjoy intercourse as much as they might because they see it as something to be accomplished—an act, even a task, to be performed—rather than a pleasure to be enjoyed. If a woman does not feel like having an orgasm because she is tired, or if a man finds he is unable, from time to time, to keep his penis erect and to ejaculate, it need be no great thing. A loving exchange of feelings is good even if only one, or neither, of the partners has an orgasm.

You may have seen dogs or other animals mating and wondered whether the position they use—the male's penis entering the female from behind—is also used by men and women. Generally it is not. There are many positions in human intercourse, and the most common one is for the partners to lie face to face, with the man above the woman. But couples can enjoy a variety of pleasures by trying out different positions and different ways of enjoying sexual satisfaction.

If a woman wants to avoid difficulty and discomfort the first time she has intercourse, she may use tampons beforehand to dilate—enlarge—the opening in her hymen, or she may enlarge it gradually over a period of time by using her fingers. She should be sure they are clean. In a few women the hymen is so strong and the opening so small that a doctor will think it wise to enlarge the vaginal entrance before the woman has intercourse. This is a simple and almost painless procedure.

Often, but not always, the first time a woman has intercourse, the stretching of the hymenal opening may cause discomfort and slight bleeding. This is physically harmless.

Chapter 8 will tell you more about human sex and compare it to sex in other animals, for one is very different from the other, and it is important to understand the differences.

5

Heredity: What Is Passed On to Us by the Sperm and the Egg

Remember that two hundred egg cells placed side by side would take up only an inch; five hundred sperm cells lined up head to tail would measure the same length. Yet each of these microscopically small cells contains many little bodies called **chromosomes,** which transmit a complicated **code** of directions. This code determines the **heredity** of the child that will be born if a sperm and an egg unite: the color of the hair, skin, and eyes; the shape of the nose; intelligence at birth; and the thousands of other things that make this human being physically different from all other human beings. You know that children often look like their parents. All the resemblance is carried by the chromosomes in a single sperm and a single egg.

For a moment, let's consider in more detail how this code of heredity is carried. Scientists are making amazing discoveries about this process. In each sperm cell and egg cell, small as each is, there are molecules of a chemical called DNA. Each molecule looks somewhat like a twisted ladder, weighs about one ten-trillionth (1/10,000,000,000,000) of an ounce, and contains many **genes.** In the genes of the DNA molecule is stored a set of chemical directions so complicated that to write them down in English would require several hundred volumes the size of the dictionary. Every cell in your body contains these molecules. They are so small that if all the

DNA molecules in all of the cells in all of the over three billion people now on the earth were piled close together like logs of wood, the whole pile would fit into a cubical box with an edge less than 1/8 of an inch, like this:

You might say that, in a sense, all the people in the world in miniature could fit into that little box.

The science of heredity is called **genetics**(from the word **gene**), and what you are now and will become is determined partly by your genes and partly by your surroundings, called **environment**. There is more about this in later chapters.

6

From Fertilization
to the Birth of the Baby

At the man's climax in intercourse, millions of sperm cells, swimming in semen, are ejaculated from his penis into the woman's vagina near the mouth of the cervix. At once, these microscopic sperm, their tails moving rapidly back and forth, begin a journey that takes from one to several hours. In their warm, moist environment, the sperm normally stay alive and are capable of fertilizing the egg cell for two and a half to three days, although sperm may be actively moving as long as a week after they are ejaculated.

Sperm appear to have no sense of direction, and of course they cannot see. They move about rapidly in a random motion, not on a direct route. Some make their way up through the cervix (see the diagram on page 6) into the uterus. Some of these enter the two fallopian

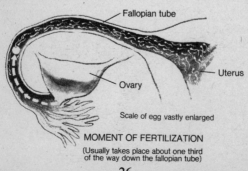

MOMENT OF FERTILIZATION
(Usually takes place about one third
of the way down the fallopian tube)

26

tubes. They proceed up the tubes, where they may meet a mature egg cell traveling slowly in the opposite direction. If they do, they crowd around the ovum and bombard its wall until it weakens at one spot just enough to permit a single sperm cell to enter. At once the cell wall hardens and the other sperm are shut out; the successful one loses its tail; its head joins the nucleus of the egg. The rest of the sperm cells die and are absorbed harmlessly into the woman's body. The moment of joining of sperm and egg is called **fertilization** or **conception;** new life is **conceived,** that is to say, begun.

It is important to understand that fertilization will not occur every time a man and woman have intercourse; far from it. The sperm must arrive in the fallopian tube just when an egg is traveling through it. The sperm must be vigorous and the egg not too old—that is, not more than twelve to twenty-four hours out of the ovary.

It is the sperm cell that determines whether the child is to be a boy or a girl. The sex depends on which of two types of sperm cell enters the ovum. If it is a sperm carrying a "Y" chromosome, the baby will be a boy; if it is an "X" chromosome, it will be a girl. Nothing that happens to the mother after fertilization can change the sex of the baby.

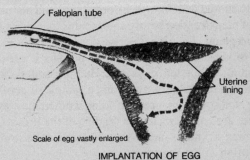

Fallopian tube

Uterine lining

Scale of egg vastly enlarged

IMPLANTATION OF EGG
IN LINING OF UTERUS

There is still no simple way for the doctor to tell for sure before birth whether the baby will be a boy or a girl. However, after the egg has been developing for about fourteen weeks, a doctor can by means of a needle with a thin tube in it draw out a small sample of the fluid surrounding the baby (called **amniotic fluid**). Amniotic fluid contains cells of the baby, cells cast off by the skin or lining of the mouth. Studying the cells to see whether there are two X chromosomes or only one X and a Y will reveal the sex of the unborn child. However, this procedure involves a small health risk and is not undertaken unless there is some urgent medical reason that requires a doctor to take a sample of the amniotic fluid. One such reason would be to determine if there is a serious defect in the development of the **fetus**—the growing unborn baby—which might result in such severe mental retardation or deformity that an abortion would be advised.

Since the thick lining of the uterus now is needed for the fertilized egg to implant itself and grow in, it is not discarded, and there are no more menstrual periods until after the baby is born. Missing her period is usually the first sign to a woman that she may be going to have a baby. However, there are other reasons for delayed or missed periods, such as fatigue, excitement, nervousness, or change of diet or climate. Therefore, a woman usually should wait for a week or two beyond her normal time of menstruation before she decides that she is probably **pregnant.** Then if her period does not come, she will want to know for sure whether or not she is pregnant. Beginning about ten days after her missed period, a doctor can tell for sure by testing a sample of her urine. Other signs of pregnancy that some women may show a bit later are enlargement and tingling of the breasts, and "morning sickness," when they feel sick at the stomach, most often in the morning.

Once a woman is pregnant, her ovaries produce no more mature eggs until after the baby is born. Thus, when a woman has intercourse during pregnancy, no egg is there ready to be fertilized by a sperm.

Let's go back for a moment to the instant of fertilization. As soon as the egg is fertilized, it begins to divide and grow as it is moved on down the fallopian tube. As you know, it enters the uterus, and after a while implants itself in the uterine wall. This whole process takes several days.

The uterus, as you have read in Chapter 2, is ready to nourish the egg as it grows. Later, with increase in size, the growing baby becomes surrounded by two strong coverings and cushioned in fluid, which protects it from jolts and shocks.

The time between conception and birth of the baby is called the period of **gestation.** The baby grows inside the womb of its mother. This is the period during which the mother is said to be **pregnant.** In human beings, pregnancy, or gestation, averages 266 days, or about eight and a half months, from the moment of fertilization, and 280 days, or nine months, from the beginning of the last menstrual period. The baby, first called an **embryo,** later a **fetus,** grows by **cell division,** from one cell at conception to over 200 billion cells at the time of birth. It is nourished by the mother by means of a thick, disc-shaped collection of blood vessels called the **placenta.** This is connected with the growing embryo by means of a long, ropelike cord, the **umbilical cord.** Through the blood vessels in this cord the embryo receives food and oxygen and disposes of waste products like carbon dioxide, but the mother's blood does **not** enter the embryo. The embryo manufactures its own blood.

The human embryo at first resembles embryos of other animals. For a short time it has the beginning of gills, as in fish embryos, although they are not really gills; later it appears to have a tail; still later its body is covered with fine, downy hair.

At four weeks the embryo is about ¼ inch long (as long as this: —— but somewhat curled). It no longer has gill-like ridges, but still has a tail; and it would be difficult to tell it apart from the embryo of a fish, turtle, chicken, or any other animal.

At eight weeks the embryo is about 1 inch long, and it would take about five hundred such embryos to weigh a pound. Even though it is this small, it already has a large-looking head with the beginnings of eyes, ears, a nose, and a mouth. Its heart is now pumping blood through its small body.

At twelve weeks the embryo has made a great spurt of growth and is now about 4 inches long, although it weighs only about ⅓ ounce—about fifty embryos to a pound.

At sixteen to seventeen weeks it has grown to be 6 inches long and weighs ⅓ pound. Its bones have begun to develop, and its arms and legs can move. The mother may now be able to feel the first faint flutter of activity inside her, called quickening. When she feels this she knows with a new certainty that a live being is inside her. By this time the being is called a fetus, no longer an embryo.

At twenty-one weeks the fetus would be about 10 inches long if its legs were stretched out straight, and it weighs about ¾ pound. Its body is now covered with downy hair.

At twenty-five weeks the fetus is about a foot long and weighs perhaps 1¼ pounds. It is beginning to lose the hair that covered its body and looks quite a lot like a baby now, except that it is thin and has not yet begun to store up fat.

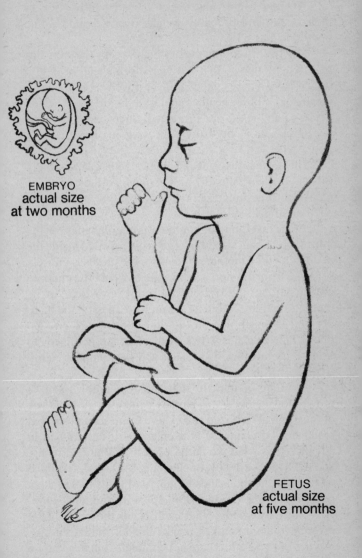

EMBRYO
actual size
at two months

FETUS
actual size
at five months

At about twenty-nine weeks—seven months—it is 14 inches long and probably weighs over 2 pounds. The body hair has all gone.

(By twenty-four to twenty-eight weeks the baby has matured enough so that if it were born ahead of time it would have a bare chance to live, if well cared for in an **incubator,** a little, heated, enclosed, boxlike bed which keeps a baby warm and protected. Such a baby is called **premature,** as is any baby born weighing less that 5 ½ pounds.)

During months eight and nine the fetus grows rapidly to an average weight of 7 or 8 pounds. At the end of the nine-month gestation period, it is ready to be born, all 200 billion cells of it.

In the last three or four months of pregnancy, as the fetus increases in size, things get a bit crowded inside the abdomen of the mother. Of course, the uterus is entirely separate from the stomach (in spite of what little children are sometimes told about the baby growing "in its mother's tummy"), but as the uterus expands, the bladder and stomach and all the other organs are pressed upon. That explains why an expectant mother needs to urinate more often than usual and eats smaller, more frequent meals.

It seems a miracle that the remarkable plan of growth for the body was already contained in the DNA of the original fertilized cell. There was a **set pattern** that could not be changed. Not only was it determined in advance that what would be born was a human being, and not a mouse or cow or elephant, but also determined were all of the thousands of inherited traits that make a person truly the product of his parents and ancestors.

You may wonder what the effect on the fetus is if the pregnant woman smokes, drinks alcohol, or takes drugs. Studies of these effects are not complete, but it is known that mothers who smoke tend to have smaller babies

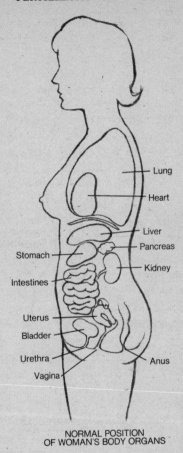

Lung

Heart

Liver

Pancreas

Stomach

Kidney

Intestines

Uterus

Bladder

Urethra

Anus

Vagina

NORMAL POSITION
OF WOMAN'S BODY ORGANS

(this is not to say less healthy ones) than those who do
not. Also, when the mother smokes, the heartbeat of the
fetus speeds up somewhat. When the mother drinks
alcohol, the baby's movements inside the uterus are
slowed down while the alcohol is in the mother's bloodstream, but this does not harm the baby as far as we
know. Marijuana also has a temporary effect on the baby

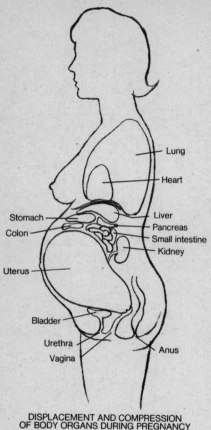

DISPLACEMENT AND COMPRESSION
OF BODY ORGANS DURING PREGNANCY

but not a harmful one. However, the drug heroin can be very injurious to the baby. As the mother becomes addicted to heroin, the baby also becomes addicted, and after it is born it goes through painful and serious withdrawal symptoms, just as an adult does when taken off the drug.

One birth in every ninety or so produces twins.

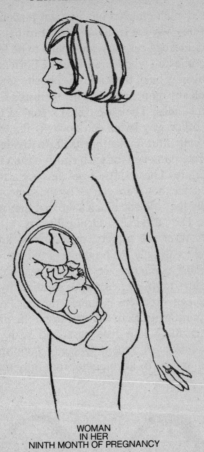

WOMAN
IN HER
NINTH MONTH OF PREGNANCY

(One in about every eight thousand produces triplets.)
Twins are formed in two ways. One is that each of the
mother's two ovaries releases an egg at about the same
time, or one ovary releases two eggs. Thus, each fallopian tube contains an egg, or one tube contains two eggs,
and, when the sperm cells enter the tubes, both eggs are
fertilized. Each egg becomes separately implanted in the

uterus, and each embryo has its own placenta. Twins who start this way are really ordinary brothers or sisters whose original egg cells just happened to be fertilized at the same time and who were therefore born at the same time. They may be of the same or opposite sex, and they do not look any more alike than brothers and sisters born at different times. They are called **fraternal twins.**

The other way twins can occur is for the original fertilized cell, after implanting itself, to divide once into two separate parts and for each embryo then to develop independently. These single-egg twins are always of the same sex since they were started by the same sperm cell, and usually they look so much alike that they are hard to tell apart. They are called **identical twins.**

Much rarer are triplets, quadruplets, and quintuplets, who are usually the products of two or more eggs. Triplets most commonly result from two eggs, one of which divides to produce a pair of identical twins, while the other egg produces a single infant. The famous Dionne quintuplets were thought to be the products of one egg dividing into five parts, all with the same placenta. The more recent Diligenti quintuplets from Argentina appear to have come from only three eggs.

FRATERNAL TWINS
From two eggs;
two placentas;
sexes may differ

IDENTICAL TWINS
From one egg, divided;
single placenta;
sexes the same

7

How a Baby Is Born
and What a Newborn Is Like

In just a little less than nine months after the baby is conceived (the egg fertilized), it is ready to be born. The mother's first signal that the time for birth has come is usually the start of **contractions** of the strong muscles of the uterus, accompanied by a dull ache or sensation of tightening as the contractions increase in power. (All muscles do their work by contracting.) At first these contractions are spaced perhaps fifteen minutes to half an hour apart, but when they begin to come every five to ten minutes, the mother should be taken to the hospital, or the doctor or **midwife** who will help her with the birth should be called in. (A doctor who specializes in delivering children is called an **obstetrician;** a midwife is a person, usually a nurse, especially trained to help in childbirth.)

The muscular contractions are called **labor,** and a woman who is about to bear a child is said to be **in labor.** There is no doubt that giving birth to a child is hard work. It can also be painful, but much of the discomfort can be avoided by the expectant mother who has conditioned her body for childbirth (there are training courses available to help provide this conditioning) and who understands well enough what is happening during birth so that she can help guide the process.

The discomfort of a woman in childbirth is perfectly natural, being caused by the powerful muscles which

BIRTH OF BABY

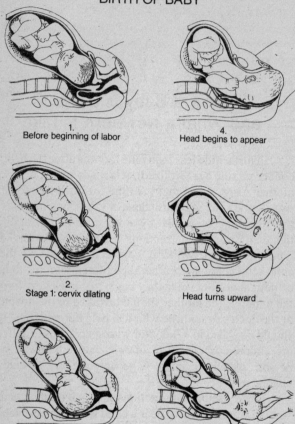

1.
Before beginning of labor

4.
Head begins to appear

2.
Stage 1: cervix dilating

5.
Head turns upward

3.
Beginning of Stage 2:
cervix completely dilated

6.
Birth of shoulders

push out the baby. Many women prefer to have an anesthetic, which relieves the discomfort. Other women would rather be fully conscious while bearing a child, with only a mild anesthetic or none at all. Understanding what the experience of childbirth involves can relieve fear and anxiety, and this relief helps relax the muscles around the vagina, and particularly the cervix, which must dilate, or stretch, to permit passage of the baby. Understanding makes the mother more relaxed, which increases the ease of the birth and helps speed the arrival of the baby.

The average length of labor for a mother producing her first child is between nine and eleven hours from the time the first regular contractions are felt; but some babies come much more quickly, others more slowly. The time for mothers who have already given birth is usually shorter, averaging around six hours.

Usually, during good labor, the covering membranes which enclosed the baby break by themselves, and the water they contained, which had acted as a cushion for the baby, flows out through the vagina. Sometimes labor is progressing well but the membranes haven't broken by themselves. In such cases the doctor uses a little clamp painlessly to pinch an opening so that the fluid will come out and the period of labor be shortened. After this "rush of waters," as it is called, and toward the end of labor, the baby is rather quickly transported through the vagina and out into the world by a series of pushes by the uterus. The head usually comes first, and is usually a tight fit. But at the time of birth the baby's head is compressible enough not to be damaged, and it serves well to open the way for the rest of the body. The doctor or midwife is waiting to guide the head gently as it emerges and to guide the baby out easily as the birth is completed. After a minute or so, the doctor ties and cuts the umbilical cord. This process is painless, since the cord contains no nerves. Your **navel,** or belly button, is the small scar that shows where the umbilical cord that linked you to the placenta inside your mother was attached to you.

After the baby is born, the uterus goes on contract-

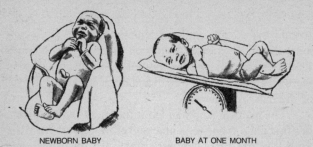

NEWBORN BABY   BABY AT ONE MONTH

ing, but less vigorously, and in a few minutes the placenta and the two coverings that were protecting the baby emerge. These are called the **afterbirth** and are disposed of.

At birth the baby is for the first time on his own, and his first job is to start breathing in air—something he did not need to do and could not do floating in fluid inside the uterus. Sometimes it is helpful for the doctor to suction out the baby's nose and throat with a rubber bulb syringe or a suction machine to make it easier for him to start breathing. After his first breaths he is likely to utter a small, high cry, which is a delightful signal to the mother that she has produced a child. What an accomplishment! A new life begins.

Many boys and girls, having seen babies a few weeks or months old and knowing how cute and pretty they look, are a bit disappointed and even shocked when they see a newborn baby. (So are mothers and fathers.) Usually a newborn is not at all beautiful, or even cute. He is wrinkly, splotchy, and often quite red. The baby's face may be swollen and look troubled, stupid, or even worn out, and in general he doesn't seem to be much of an addition to the family. But we have to remember that the process of getting himself born may have been fairly hard on him. However, his color soon becomes normal, and his skin gets to look more skinlike. In less than a month he will be a cute and desirable-looking baby, and even a day or two after birth can work wonders.

A newborn can see enough to tell light from dark, but things are blurry to him at first until his eyes get used to focusing. He can taste, and he can feel pain and pressure. He does not like loud noises or the sensation of falling. He quickly learns that the way to get what he needs is to cry. Many babies do a lot of crying during the first month, whether they need something or not.

An activity the newborn does very well is sucking. He has very strong sucking muscles and a little pad of fat in each cheek to help him. He will suck on anything that is put near his mouth. His mother has just the right equipment for him to suck on. At the end of each of her breasts is a **nipple,** and inside the breasts are glands that manufacture milk and a network of small tubes that bring the milk to the nipple when the baby sucks.

For the first day or two after the birth, the fluid from the mother's breasts, called **colostrum,** is slight in amount, yellowish, and watery. This is just what the baby needs: it contains some food and also special sub-

stances that protect him from possible infections to which he is exposed now that he is in the world. The baby sucks actively even though he doesn't get much, and such sucking stimulates the breast glands to make milk that is more nutritious.

Mother's milk is an ideal baby food: it is clean, safe, and digestible, with just the right proportions of protein, fats, carbohydrates, minerals, and vitamins. Being held close and nursing at his mother's breast continues for a baby the feeling of warmth and closeness to his mother that he needs, and it is also pleasant and healthy for the mother, too.

There are a good many mothers who do not wish, or do not feel able, to nurse their babies. These babies are fed from a bottle that has a rubber nipple and contains a special formula similar to breast milk, and they grow to be as sturdy and healthy as a breast-fed baby, especially if the mother or father holds the baby in her or his arms lovingly while the child sucks from the bottle.

8

Human Sex and Animal Sex: Some Major Differences

The main function of sex in nature is **reproduction,** that is, producing babies and carrying on the species, whether the species be birds, bees, rabbits, hamsters, hippopotamuses, gorillas, or human beings. Nothing in nature could be more important, and that is why sex is so attractive and the drive for it so urgent.

However, there are important differences between sex in animals and sex in human beings. One difference is this: in most animals, **copulation** or mating usually takes place only when the female is **in heat**—that is, as she is ovulating and when copulation will produce pregnancy. When she is in heat, she gives forth a certain scent or other sign which tells the male she is ready to copulate. The male then becomes sexually aroused (he "ruts" or becomes "rutty"), and the mating takes place. At no other time is the female willing to copulate, and usually only at that time is the male responsive. Thus, the main result of copulation in animals is reproduction. Of course, animals do not "know" this. They copulate because they feel an urge to do so.

In human females, on the other hand, there is no such thing as heat. Most women usually do not even know when they have ovulated and have an egg that is ready to be fertilized. They do feel a greater desire for intercourse at some times than at others, but not necessarily at the time when they are most likely to conceive.

Women do not give forth any special scent; their bodies do not advertise their readiness, as do animal bodies. Further, the human male is more or less always ready for sexual activity. There is no definite season when he is "rutty."

Thus, human sexual desire has relatively little relationship to whether or not a baby is likely to be produced at a given time. Most sexual intercourse between human beings takes place because of the desire, pleasure, joy, and love that are a part of it, rather than because of the need to produce children.

Furthermore, animal copulation and human intercourse are quite different, as different as animal eating is from human meals. Most healthy animals gobble their food quickly when they are hungry. They aren't concerned with whether the food looks good or they are comfortable with the people at the table. They eat solely because they are hungry. If another animal comes around, they may try to drive the intruder away.

But human beings enjoy eating together. There may be interesting conversation; the table can be a center of affection and pleasure. According to different national customs, there are different rules of behavior toward other people; and there can be beauty, too, in the way the food is presented, the way the room and the table are decorated, and how the people look.

Sexual intercourse between a man and a woman, as I have said, can be and often is a beautiful, loving, joyous thing. If the couple care for each other, their physical pleasure and sense of deep relationship can give them real ecstasy. On the other hand, it is not always so, and much depends on how the couple are feeling toward each other at the time and how they feel about their own lives. It depends quite a lot also on their surroundings. That's why I stated that most animal sex is as different from human sex as animal eating is from human meals.

The basic difference between human and animal sex arises out of the facts that I have described. Human beings **decide** when they are going to engage in sexual activity; most animals have the decision made for them by instinct, by what is born into them, not by what is learned or thought about. **Human beings are responsible for their sex life;** animals are not. There is great variation in human sex life, variation from country to country, from culture to culture, from group to group, from person to person. There is no such variation within a species of animals; dogs mate in the same way whether they are in India, France, Haiti, or the United States. Animal sex is only a matter of body; human sex involves the personality, the mind, and the emotions—and the upbringing, too.

And there is yet another major difference. When animals in nature become sexually mature, they begin at once to copulate and reproduce their kind. And when young are produced by animals, the period during which the parents must provide care for them is generally quite short, usually less than a year. For example, with dogs and cats it is only several weeks, whereas human beings are responsible for the care of their young from fifteen to twenty years, or more—longer than any animal. Even after human beings reach puberty, it may still be eight to ten years, or even longer in our culture, before they are ready to earn a living, establish a home, and take care of children of their own— in other words, to be responsible for the possible consequences of intercourse. This is something that boys and girls need to think about. (See Chapter 13, "Contraception.") There's much more to parenthood than having a cute little baby to love, be loved by, and be proud of.

Let me repeat: an animal has little sexual freedom; it is limited by its season and driven by its instincts to copulate almost automatically. For it, the patterns are all set up in advance; there is little learning or choice. An animal's sex life is primarily for reproduction. But men and women have much freedom of choice; they must decide what to do and what not to do; they depend on good teaching and good learning. **Men and women are responsible for their choices and decisions:** they must take the consequences, good or bad. Therefore, it is extremely important that they have enough knowledge, sense, and consideration to foresee those consequences and to act accordingly.

Thus, human love and sex can result in pleasure and joyous satisfaction. Or the result can be a great sorrow and unhappiness, if men and women in their sex lives are not considerate of each other and do not take responsibility for the results.

9

Sex Differences
Between Men and Women
—and Some Similarities

We are now ready to go more deeply into the subject of sex differences between men and women—into human **sexuality.** Sexuality means more than sex. It means all that goes with being a man or being a woman. It means a person's sexual nature. Authorities who have studied sex differences do not agree on the extent to which they are **inborn** or are created by the **environment,** that is, the society we live in.

Before we think about differences between men and women, we should remember that there are at least two great similarities: First, as **human beings,** we are much more like each other than we are like any other animal of either sex. We speak and write language, we think complicated thoughts, we can remember tha past and project ourselves into the future, we have imagination, we enjoy planning and loving and seeing ourselves as parts of the universe. Both male and female human beings are **self-conscious** and **other-conscious** in ways that no other animals are. And the second great similarity is physical: Again as human beings, both men and women can enjoy varieties of sexual activity and the ultimate sexual pleasure of orgasm with a degree of conscious awareness that animals, as far as we know, do not have.

As for the differences, when we compare the sexuality of men and women, it is important to remember that a woman is more than just a nonman, and a man is more than just a nonwoman, and that every woman is different from every other woman, and every man different from every other man.

Sexuality in Men. When a boy has matured sexually, the sexual thoughts in his mind and feelings in his body are quite definite and strong. They may be aroused at any time and rather quickly, and the arousal may be quite involuntary. The physical feelings are strongest in his penis and may sometimes make him desire an ejaculation.

However, most erections end without ejaculation. As boys grow up, many of them come to understand that a sexual experience like intercourse is not something to be sought lightly or selfishly. When it is part of an expression of tenderness and caring, it can be a deeply stirring experience. Boys and men can combine their intelligence, their emotions, and their sexuality to help create relationships based on love, understanding, and caring. Girls can, too.

Sexuality in Women. A woman's sexuality tends to be somewhat different from a man's. Generally her sexual feelings are stirred more slowly, less often, and less sharply than those of men. However, once aroused, her feelings are very powerful and very pleasurable. For a woman, sex is usually a response to love or to a romantic feeling in addition to specific excitation. Also, it is a way to express her love. But she expresses it in many ways besides intercourse. Thus, women want intercourse less at some times than at others, yet it is especially important to most of them always to give and receive love and affection as a part of lovemaking.

The sexual nature of women helps to make them understanding, considerate, and affectionate, and it is a great force in creating deep and satisfying human relationships. The sexual nature of men can well do the same.

Too often a man thinks that a woman reacts—or should react—just as he does; and a woman does not understand the speed and power of a man's reaction. Understanding their sexual differences and lovingly considering them will help a man and a woman to be happy together. Many years ago it was widely thought that men were supposed to enjoy sex and women were supposed to endure it. There are still some people who believe a woman is not quite "nice" if she really enjoys sex. But ever since the 1920s people have come increasingly to understand that women and men both can enjoy intense sexual pleasure, that sex is not something that a man does **to** an woman or that a woman does **for** a man. A woman's orgasm is as strong and definite and exciting as a man's ejaculation, and may be even more so. Also, her orgasm may last longer than a man's, and she may have several orgasms in rather quick succession, which a man cannot have. Intercourse at its best is a mutual exchange of pleasure.

Sexuality Is More Than Bodies. Boys and girls, and men and woman, express their sexuality in many different ways. Sexual intercourse, including the steps leading up to it, is only one of the ways. Other ways are: clothing, conversation, manners, interests, education, recreation, daily work, and most details of life. A person does what he does as a person, yes, but also as a boy or a girl, or as a man or a woman.

If you think back into your early childhood, you will probably remember that your parents treated you as a boy or as a girl, not only as a person. The words they spoke to you, the toys they gave you, the games they played with you, the clothes they dressed you in, the things they punished and rewarded you for—all of these

things and many more—helped develop the way you
express yourself sexually, helped to establish your
gender identity, whether you consider yourself to be
male or female, helped to make you a boy or a girl with
what is generally accepted as the personality of a boy or
girl.

Men and women tend to differ, therefore, in their
feelings, desires, and personalities largely because they
have been **taught** these differences. They may not be as
quickly obvious as the differences in their bodies, but
they are deep-seated and important. In general, until
fairly recently, anyway, most people have thought of a
typical boy as vigorous and aggressive, of a typical girl as
sweeter and gentler than he and with a greater desire to
please others. A father has been expected to earn a living
for his family and to provide manly companionship for
his wife and children. On the other hand, a mother, even
when she helps earn a living for the family, as so many
women now do, is expected to provide loving care for
her children, to manage the household, and to be a
source of tenderness and womanly love. Men and
women go well together in this way. And when they do,
the result is a delight.

In recent years, however, there has been a strong
desire on the part of many boys and girls and men and
women not to be so molded by these expected **sex
roles**—our society's ideas of how male and female ought
to behave. Increasingly, we have come to accept hus-
bands and wives sharing more equally the tasks of making a living and making a home. We recognize that some
girls are aggressive and ambitious and some boys are
gentle and accepting and that this is all right. People have
come more and more to want to be free, free to be
themselves, whichever sex they may belong to. They are
less willing to play unthinkingly the role of man or woman
that our society encourages. In other words, we are

coming to see that in each of us there is some of what we think of as the masculine and some of what we think of as the feminine. This is fortunate because it makes it easier for men and women to understand each other. I want to emphasize that most of us have more similarities as human beings than we have differences as men and women. Some will find satisfaction and pleasure in living the sexual roles that society has traditionally expected of us. Others will find new ways of relating that are more satisfying to us.

Obviously, however, body differences do make substantial differences in the lives of men and women, expecially those who marry and have families. The woman is the one who goes through the period of pregnancy and who gives birth to the baby; the man can't. The woman is the only one who can nurse the baby, if the baby is to be breast-fed. For thousands of years, these body differences between men and women have made an overriding difference in their lives. Woman became pregnant frequently, they were tied to their primitive homes, they had no choice but to carry, bear, and care for children. The men, on the other hand, were the ones who could be counted on to go out on cooperative hunting expeditions and bring home the food the tribe and family needed. Thus, over thousands of years the pattern of man, the hunter, and woman, the homebody, developed. Despite modern developments I have mentioned, this pattern remains the most common one the world over.

There is another way that body differences cause men and women to differ. This is in the chemicals, called **hormones,** that the glands in men's and women's bodies secrete into their bloodstreams. This subject is very complicated and not yet fully understood, but, to take just one example, it is known that men's testicles secrete a hormone called **testosterone,** and that this hormone causes not only the so-called **secondary sex characteristics** like the beard and a larger, stronger body of a man, but also helps to cause vigorous behavior. Women's bodies also manufacture testosterone (the adrenal glands, which both men and women have, are the manufacturers), but normally much less of it than does the body of the typical male.

So the long history of the human race, the different proportions of hormones in men's and women's bodies, and the facts of pregnancy and childbirth, result in certain inescapable differences in men and women. But these differences, which used to rule our lives, are no longer nearly as powerful as they were. Modern civilization has made it possible for both men and women to be more free to become the sort of people they want to be, with much less forced dependence on sexual and physical differences.

It is often difficult for us to know how to deal with our sexual feelings, whether toward people of the opposite sex or toward those of our own sex. It may also be difficult to deal with questions we may have about our gender identity and how to express it. None of us, and expecially no young person, should hesitate to discuss with a knowledgeable person our sexual feelings if we would like to understand them better or are bothered by them and would like to try to change them. We should never have to feel "stuck" with our problems or with emotions that cause us discomfort.

10

Homosexuality——Being "Gay"

Some people prefer sexual partners of their own sex and are not sexually attracted to the other sex (although, like anyone else, they may be attracted to people of either sex in many ways other than sexual). Such people are called **homosexual.** They often refer to themselves, and are referred to, as "gay." Most homosexuals look no different from anyone else unless they choose, as some do at times, to look, dress, and act differently.

The work "homosexual" means "having to do with the same sex." (The first part of the word comes from the Greek *homos,* meaning "same," not from the Latin *homo,* meaning "man.") The opposite of homosexual is **heterosexual,** "having to do with the other sex or with both sexes" (from the Greek *heteros,* "other"). Heterosexuals are called "straight," as distinguished from "gay." Female homosexuals are often called **lesbians.** The name comes from the Greek island of Lesbos, where, in ancient times, many of the inhabitants were women who enjoyed a homosexual way of life together.

There are many people who are not homosexual or heterosexual in the complete sense, but are **bisexual** (*bi-*comes from Latin and means "having to do with two"). They are people who can go either way, heterosexual or homosexual.

People often ask: What causes some individuals to prefer homosexual love and others to prefer heterosexual? Because of the present incomplete state of our knowledge, there is as yet no answer or single theory on which all scientists and doctors agree. There is fairly general agreement, however, that our preferences are for the most part established in the first few years of our lives and have to do with how we are treated by our parents and others very close to us.

Some boys and girls when they enter puberty, or even earlier, feel strongly attracted to members of their own sex. For a while, most boys usually much prefer to associate with other boys, and girls with other girls. With some, these friendships are close and intense. They occasionally involve sexual experiences such as kissing or caressing, or masturbating together. Such experiences in most cases do not mean that those who participate in them are homosexuals. Most adolescents who engage in them go on to form heterosexual relationships.

Sometimes, also, a younger boy develops a special, intense fondness for a man, perhaps a teacher or a coach, or an older boy. Some girls experience the same sort of feeling toward a woman or older girl whom they admire. (Such a feeling is sometimes called a "crush.") It is usually a one-way feeling; the older person probably does not feel the same way and may even be unaware of the special emotion of the younger person. Ordinarily, after a time, the boy or girl develops other interests and the intense feeling passes. This feeling of warm admiration for a more mature person of the same sex can have a beneficial effect on the development of the character and personality of a young teen-ager, if it leads him or her to strive for the admired qualities.

It is impossible to say how many people would openly express themselves through a mainly homosexual style of life if they felt perfectly free to do so. Perhaps as many as 10 percent would, and probably more men than women. As it is, many people know that they are homosexual but feel forced to try to hide it from the rest of the world. The reason for this is that, commonly, life for homosexuals in the present state of our society is made difficult because so many people unthinkingly condemn homosexuality as strange and abnormal and reject those who practice it. This condemnation and rejection make it difficult for many homosexuals to have good feelings about themselves. Also, it is more difficult for homosexuals than for others to get good jobs or to be accepted as friends by heterosexual people. Those who discriminate against homosexuals in this way are displaying what is sometimes called **homophobia:** a strong, unreasoning fear of homosexuality. It is not unlike racial or religious prejudice. Despite the effects of homophobia in our society, however, many homosexual and bisexual men and women are happy and satisfied and are managing to make successes of their lives. They are found in all walks of life—the sciences, engineering, construction work, the arts, sports, and business management, to mention only a few.

Homosexual leaders and many others use the slogan "Gay is good." They have recently organized into hundreds of groups around the country, some on school and college campuses. Together, these groups are known as the gay liberation movement. This movement encourages homosexuals to "come out," freely to enjoy their style of life, and to fight discrimination against homosexuals.

Gay people feel that they should be allowed to express themselves just as heterosexuals are allowed to do—by holding hands in public, dancing together at a party, or introducing their family to someone they love. But they find that it takes great courage in our antihomosexual society for them to do these simple, human things. They say that homosexuality is not a problem in itself, but that the problem lies in the bigotry and discrimination that gay men and women face, and they urge all people, straight and gay, to uphold the right of gay people, along with all people, to live in ways that are fulfilling for them and harmless to others.

11

Masturbation

Masturbation—boys often call it "jacking off" or "jerking off"—means rubbing or stroking the genitals in order to have an orgasm. A boy does it by rubbing his penis, especially the head of the penis, with his hand or perhaps with or against some other object; a girl does it by stroking her clitoris or the area around it or by pressing her thighs together rhythmically. Masturbation begins when very young children learn that they get a pleasurable feeling by handling their genitals. However, it is not limited to the young. Many men and women go on masturbating from time to time throughout the sexually active period of their lives. Both married and unmarried people masturbate, and people can masturbate alone or together, homosexually or heterosexually. Although there is certainly nothing wrong with **not** masturbating, the person who has never masturbated is an exception.

People often talk and write about masturbation as a problem of sex. It really isn't a problem except as thinking makes it so. Unfortunately, many people **believe** that masturbation is harmful and are deeply worried about boys and girls who masturbate. This is especially true among people who belong to a religious group that considers it to be a sin. If a young person who masturbates lives closely with others who believe it is evil, he will probably feel guilty and ashamed. And, of course, when babies or very little girls or boys are punished for playing with their genitals, this fixes in their minds the idea that it's a bad thing.

Then there are those who say that masturbation may not be so bad if you don't do it too much—whatever that means. It's really impossible to masturbate too much because when your body has had enough it will no longer respond to such efforts to have an orgasm. However, given the strong feelings most people have about the privacy of sex, it is wise to masturbate only in private. Little children don't know this, which partly explains why they get punished for a harmless activity.

I think it will be useful for me to state some facts about masturbation, just to help remove any fears you or your parents may have. Masturbation is harmless to the body. It does not cause mental illness (although it can be followed by a damaging sense of guilt and shame in people brought up to fear it); it does not lessen a person's later capacity to enjoy sex in marriage. The stories about its causing pimples, circles under the eyes, weakness, or various diseases are just plain myths and not to be taken seriously.

Masturbation is a source of sexual pleasure. You get no diseases from it, and nobody ever became pregnant by masturbating. It serves to release sexual tension which otherwise may push people into having sexual intercourse before they are emotionally ready for it or any of its possible consequences. In addition, masturbation can provide an outlet for a person's sexual imagination and daydreaming. Some boys and girls are very worried about the thoughts they have while they masturbate, and at many other times. They should not be, for sexual fantasies of all kinds are common, more so than uninformed people believe.

Masturbation can help a boy or man learn how to delay his ejaculation and prolong his erection during a period of sexual stimulation. Then later on, when he is ready for marriage and the intercourse that is such an important part of it, he will be less likely to ejaculate too soon, before his partner is satisfied. Also, masturbation can help a woman learn how to achieve an orgasm. She can find what makes her feel good and, when she has learned, she can communicate this to her mate so that both can enjoy the pleasure of orgasm. Many women take years to learn that they can have an orgasm, and some never do. Masturbation can help them to achieve this pleasure earlier.

12

Some Ways That Sex
Can Become a Problem

Automobiles, fire, sex—they all have power. Whether their power produces good or bad results depends on how the power is used. Automobiles are a valuable means of transportation, but they become a problem when they kill over fifty thousand Americans a year, pollute our air, and crowd our cities. Fire is essential for cooking, heating, and many industrial processes, but it becomes a problem when it destroys houses and factories, burns people, or helps launch the weapons of death. And sex, delightful and productive as it is for carrying on the human race, binding people and families together, and giving great pleasure, can also become a problem in ways that are described below.

Sex Used Selfishly

Perhaps the most common problem of sex is the misuse of sexual power or attractiveness for people's own selfish purposes without consideration of the others involved. Of course, I am not talking simply about the intense bodily pleasure that comes from orgasm and which is in many ways a self-centered pleasure, although each partner of a loving couple will care about the pleasure of the other. I am talking about the husband who insists that his wife have sex with him when she doesn't feel like it; about the girl who looks and acts supersexy just to tease a boy and then to humiliate him by refusing; about the boy who pretends to love a girl in order to win her when all he really intends to do is make a conquest and build up his own ego; about the young couples who openly display their sexual behavior even when they know (or perhaps because they know) that it makes their parents or other older people feel uncomfortable or frightened; about the boy or man who hurries a girl into sexual intercourse without troubling to understand her need as a person to feel cared for and loved, and her body's need to be made ready to respond to and enjoy the sexual experience. Sex is good when it is used considerately and understandingly, with communication; it becomes a problem when people **use** other people as mere objects for their own selfish pleasure.

Sex and Bad Feelings

Sex becomes a problem when, because of the way they were brought up or because of their experiences with sex, people develop bad feelings about it. If boys or girls have been made to believe that sex is evil, that to enjoy bodily pleasures is somehow not nice, then they will feel guilty and unhappy about their sexual desires, and it will probably take them much longer to learn to have a happy and successful sexual relationship. Of course, a couple who love and care for each other can help each other overcome such bad feelings.

Another feeling that many people suffer from is that they aren't good enough sexually. Somehow they have come to believe that sex is something to be accomplished, and the more the better. Or they have read too many foolish books and misleading advertisements, listened to too many overromantic records, and seen too many TV shows and movies based on fantasy and unrealistic expectations, and so have come to believe that if their sex life isn't a constant ecstasy, or if they and their partner don't experience an orgasm every time with heavenly bells ringing, there's something wrong with them. Or because they, like most people, don't resemble cover girls or Hollywood heroes, they feel that they can't be desirable and attractive and satisfying to the person they choose to love.

With maturity, we can gradually unlearn these feelings of inadequacy by coming to understand that **the most important thing is the quality of our relationship with the other person,** not the shape of our body or the frequency of our intercourse. There are many people who live loving lives together, with sex as an important, but not the only important, part of their lives. These people come in all shapes, sizes, colors, and varieties. But if you expect constant bliss with no effort, you are almost certainly going to feel bad about yourself and your sex life.

Adults Who Molest Children

Another problem of sex is the grown man—or, less often, woman—heterosexual or homosexual, who approaches young boys and girls and seeks sexual contact with them. Such a person might be a stranger; however, he or she might also be a family relative or someone else you know well. If you know that the possiblity of these approaches exists, you will be better prepared to deal with them. You can avoid being alone with such a person. Whether you are a boy or a girl, it is always wise for you to steer away from men or women who approach you in an overfriendly manner or who go out of their way to touch you and try to persuade you in a secret way to be alone with them.

Perhaps occasionally you have read in the newspaper about a young boy or girl being "molested" by a man. (Such a person is called a **molester**—one who molests.) This means that the man has used the young person in an attempt to satisfy his sexual desires, perhaps by exposure of his genitals, perhaps by trying to touch the genitals of the young person. People who do this sort of thing are sick and need help, but they are rarely dangerous.

If such things as these should ever happen to you, it will probably be a good idea right away to tell your parents, or someone you trust, no matter how puzzled or distressed you may feel. Tell exactly what happened; give a plain report; remember that it was not your fault. If you tell about it in this way, you may avoid being upset by the experience, and you may make it possible for the other person to receive help and be prevented from troubling other young people.

I said it would "probably" be a good idea to tell about your experience, because in some cases it might not be. Some parents or other adults get much more excited and alarmed about the situation than is justified by the plain facts. You can be reassured that most sexual contacts of molesters are quite minor and brief. This fact, and the fact that molesters seldom physically endanger the young person, are not understood by many adults. It is possible, therefore, for adults to overreact and to make the situation much more distressing than necessary to the young person who has been molested.

Rape

Newspapers often carry stories of another misuse of sex, that of **rape.** When a man rapes a woman, he forces sexual intercourse upon her, against her will. Rapists are dangerous, often filled with hate of women. They may use a gun or knife to frighten their victims and threaten to kill them if they scream or struggle. This violent, cruel use of sex is a serious crime. It may cause the woman who is raped not only to suffer pain and injury, but also cause her to be afraid of sex for a long time. She or her family should without a moment's delay inform the police so that the rapist may be caught and prevented from hurting others.

Tragic and cruel as rape is, it certainly does not mean the end of the world for the girl or woman who is raped. She will never forget it, but she can get over it, and it is especially important that she talk about it with someone, preferably with a skilled counselor, so that she may be helped. She should also consult a doctor to determine whether she might be pregnant and need an **abortion** (see p. 79).

Incest

Incest means intimate sexual relations or sexual intercourse between close relatives, such as father and daughter, mother and son, brother and sister, uncle and niece. Almost every society has strong taboos against incest, and it is considered a crime in every state in the USA. The reason commonly given for laws against incest is that any child that might result from such sexual intercourse is more likely to suffer from hereditary diseases than is a child resulting from intercourse between a couple who are not close relatives. A more important reason for condemning incest is that it often means the exploitation of a younger member of a family by an older one in a situation where the younger person is or feels trapped and finds it difficult to get help. It also can mean the upsetting of normal family relationships and making it more difficult for those involved to establish healthy sexual attachments outside the family and in marriage. A young person who finds himself or herself being forced or tempted into an incestuous relationship should at once seek help, either from another member of the family or someone outside. Of course, the parents and children in many families express their loving feelings toward each other by touching, kissing, and embracing each other. These healthy, pleasant, loving expressions are entirely different from the sexual relationships of incest.

Language and Sex

Sometimes talking about sex can become a problem. This is partly because many people think of sex as "dirty," and they think that words—especially the short, easy words—and jokes about sex are dirty. Or it may be because they feel so strongly that sex should be private, even hidden, that they believe it shouldn't be talked about. When you hear people use the expression "four-letter words," they are referring to words like *fuck*. This word is slang for sexual intercourse and comes from the Middle English word *fucken*, meaning "to strike, move quickly, penetrate." It has been a part of our language for hundreds of years. The word is objectionable to many people, and any sensitive, intelligent user of English should know this.

Of course, there is nothing essentially "dirty" about any word, for a word is merely a symbol for an idea of meaning—a sound or a group of letters. But many words do carry with them strong emotional feelings, especially words having to do with sex, and you should keep this in mind. Otherwise, you may anger and shock people and cause them to condemn you. It is important to consider the feelings of others.

An even greater problem than talking too much about sex is not talking at all about it, not being able to communicate with others about it. To enable you to communicate more easily and intelligently about sex is one of the main reasons I wrote this book.

Two other major problems connected with sex are unwanted babies and venereal disease. The next two chapters discuss these problems.

13

Contraception:
Preventing Unwanted Pregnancy

It is possible for a couple who have intercourse regularly to have a child every year, or even more often. In such a case, if the wife were twenty when she married and if she reached menopause (when her ovaries stopped producing eggs) at forty-six, the marriage would produce more than twenty-five children! There are few couples who would have enough money, physical strength, or psychological stamina to take good care of such a large family, even if they wanted it. Therefore, most married couples practive what is called **family planning, contraception,** or **birth control;** that is, they decide how many children they think they can provide for and care for and **plan** how far apart they wish to have them. Then they limit childbirth according to this plan.

In recent years, most thoughtful people have come to agree that family planning is a necessity. For many families, the arrival of an additional child may be a tragedy. It means another person to feed, clothe, and care for; and food, clothing, and care cost money—often more money than a poor or even a middle-income family can earn. Also, it is sometimes hard on the health of the mother to have another baby, especially too soon after she has had the last one.

In addition, in families that are too large to be cared for comfortably, and in which over a long period of years there is almost always an infant who should receive so much special attention, the mother, father, and other children may all suffer from the psychological strains. It is usually far better if each baby is assured of a welcome because it is planned for and wanted and its parents feel they can give it the home and loving care that it needs.

Usually even more tragic than the birth of another child to a married couple who do not want it or cannot care for it is the birth of a child to a young couple who are having sex but are not married and not ready to be married. A baby born of unmarried parents is still called **illegitimate,** a word meaning "not according to the law or the rules." This word is being applied to children less and less these days because, really, it is the parents who should be considered illegitimate, not the baby. It is no fault of the baby. It is criminally selfish for a young unmarried couple to engage in sexual intercourse without using an effective means of birth control. They are taking chances not only with their own lives and welfare, but also with the life of the baby who may be born.

There is another urgent reason for family planning. Rapidly increasing population has become perhaps our greatest world problem. As of 1973, there were more than three and a half billion people on our planet. At its present rate of increase, the world's population will reach six or seven billion by the year 2000. Thus, before long, the world's resources will not be sufficient to support all the people being born. Indeed, this situation already exists in many countries, especially in Asia, Africa, and Latin America. Therefore, the job of mankind is to learn how to limit the population to the number of people who can be well taken care of. One result of overpopulation is overwhelming competition, hunger, and disease. Another result is the overuse and pollution of the limited total supply of land, minerals, water, and air that are available to us who live on planet earth.

Especially responsible for this overuse are the people in nations with high standards of living like the United States, who consume vast quantities of resources per person. It is estimated that one average American during his lifetime will consume about thirty-five times more of the world's limited resources than will the average citizen of India.

Therefore, if we really seek a better life for all, especially we who are large consumers, we will strive to have families produce only the number of children for whom they can provide a decent standard of living and whom they can accept lovingly. This will result in a population and consumption of resources that our world can support. For a nation to have a stable population size, families will have to **average** about two children each. Now that couples are free to choose, we can expect that some will decide to have no children at all, or only one child, while an occasional couple who are mature and strong enough to handle it will choose to have a large family, thus not only maintaining the desired average but seasoning the population pot with people of varied backgrounds and experience.

There is also, of course, the possibility, for those who want more children but do not wish to increase the world's population problem, of adopting children. This can be a very rewarding experience for the parents who adopt and for the children who are adopted.

Today, the practice of contraception—or birth control—is legal in every state and accepted by every major religion in the United States. The main discussion is about what **methods of contraception** are acceptable. The Catholic church has opposed methods which it considers to be "unnatural" and thus against the will of God. It is important for all people to respect the strong moral feelings of many Catholics on this matter. It is equally important for Catholics to respect the moral feelings of those who favor various methods of contraception.

Today, Catholics see as clearly as anyone the need for family planning and the control of population and the consumption of world resources. They believe that contraception can be practiced without moral wrong if the means used are "natural." The big question for them is: What is natural?

Knowledge of methods of contraception is part of the information about sex that any intelligent person should have. **The essential thing in preventing the conception of a child is to keep a live sperm cell from joining a live egg cell and fertilizing it.** Here are the contraceptive methods most commonly used:

The "Pill"

The birth control **pill** is taken by mouth and causes chemical changes in the woman's body that stop her from ovulating. Thus, no egg is released to be fertilized. One pill a day is taken for three weeks, beginning on the fifth day after menstruation starts, and then the pills are stopped for one week, during which time a vaginal flow like menstruation takes place. The pills are usually sold in dispensers that help the woman not to forget to take her pill. Some dispensers contain a pill to be taken every day. Each space in the dispenser for the no-pill days contains a placebo pill, one that contains no chemicals. This makes it even easier never to forget to take the needed pill.

Taking a pill for only one day, or a few days, has no effect. The pills should be used only when prescribed by a doctor. They are just about 100 percent effective **if used properly.** Not a single day should be skipped. If it is,

other means of contraception must be used until the next
menstrual period begins.

Intrauterine Devices

Intrauterine devices, called IUD's, are plastic rings,
coils, loops, or other shapes, any one of which is inserted
by a doctor into the flat, triangular cavity of the uterus
and which, by means not yet entirely understood, either
prevents fertilization or keeps the egg from implanting
itself in the wall of the uterus for as long as the IUD is in
place. The IUD has a thin plastic thread attached to it
that hangs down through the cervix so that the woman
can feel it with her finger and thus make a regular check
to be sure that the IUD has not been expelled.

The advantages of the IUD are its very low cost and
the simplicity of its use, for once it has been inserted,
nothing more needs to be done except for the woman to
make an occasional checkup visit to the doctor. It is very
reliable, especially when used by women who have had a
child and whose uterine cavity is therefore permanently
somewhat enlarged and is thus less likely to expel the
IUD. The IUD is not quite as certain of success, however, as the pill.

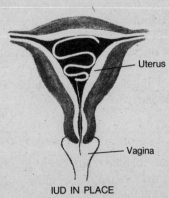

Uterus

Vagina

IUD IN PLACE

Diaphragm

A **diaphragm** is a round rubber cap, usually about 2 to 3 inches in diameter, which, before intercourse, the woman places in the vagina so as to wall off the cervix, or neck of the womb, from the main part of the vagina. It prevents the sperm from entering the cervix. It is obtained by prescription only, and must be fitted by a doctor, who instructs the woman how to insert it before intercourse. The diaphragm is used with a special kind of cream or jelly which kills sperm cells. It is somewhat less effective than the IUD.

Condom

A **condom** is a thin rubber device shaped like the finger of a glove. It is placed over the man's erect penis before intercourse and prevents the sperm from escaping into the vagina. It is often called a "rubber" or a "safe." It is available everywhere without prescription. If the condom is new, and if the man does not use it while the woman's vagina is very dry and not slippery, and if when he puts it on he leaves a small space at the end of the penis to receive the ejaculated semen, and if he carefully holds the condom in place with his fingers and withdraws his penis before he loses his erection so that no semen will spill into the vagina, then it is a very effective means of contraception. Also, there must be no continuation of intercourse without changing condoms. If condoms are carelessly or inexpertly used, they are not reliable.

Chemicals

Chemicals include a number of foams, creams, and jellies which the woman places in her vagina and which may block or kill the sperm and thus prevent fertilization of the egg. These are not nearly so effective as the methods described above, even when carefully used according to instructions, but they are better than nothing. They are available at drugstores without prescription.

Rhythm Method

The rhythm method is a method of birth control based on the possibility of a "safe period" before and after ovulation when a woman is not fertile, when she might have intercourse without conceiving a child. The theory is that if a couple have intercourse only during these safe periods, they may succeed, by a "natural" method, in limiting the number of children they have. However, science has not been able to find an easy and satisfactory way of telling just when ovulation occurs, so that for most women the rhythm method is not reliable. There is no time a woman may be sure she is absolutely "safe" during her monthly cycle, except the first three or four days of her menstrual period.

The rhythm method has been the only one up to the present approved by the Catholic Church, but high officials are studying this serious question to see if a method of contraception can be found and approved that will help members of the Roman Catholic faith. At present, many parish priests leave it up to the conscience of the Catholic couple whether or not to use the pill, and many Catholics decide to follow their own consciences without asking the Church what to do.

Withdrawl

Withdrawal is an old and commonly used method. It requires the man to withdraw his penis from the woman's vagina just before ejaculation so that the semen is deposited well away from her vagina. The withdrawal method is highly unreliable because the man may not withdraw his penis soon enough, or his penis, even before ejaculation, may secrete a small quantity of fluid containing sperm. However, it is a lot better than nothing, and it was the method used to bring birth rates down in certain countries of Europe before modern contraceptives were available.

Sterilization

Still another method sometimes used by people who wish never to have any more children involves **sterilization** of either the man or the woman in a way that prevents fertilization yet does not lessen either one's capacity to enjoy intercourse. In men this is done by means of a minor, easy, inexpensive, and harmless surgical operation. A short section from each vas deferens, the tube that carries the sperm from the testicles, is cut and the remaining ends tied. Instead of passing along the tube, the sperm are absorbed into the man's body. Thus, no sperm are contained in the semen when the man ejaculates. Since the sperm make up only a microscopically small part of the semen, no reduction in the quantity of semen is noticeable. The operation is called a **vasectomy.**

Women can be sterilized by having their fallopian tubes tied and cut by a surgeon so that egg cells cannot pass from the ovary into the uterus. This operation is called a **tubal ligation.** At present, it is a more difficult operation than a vasectomy and must be done in a hospital, though doctors have developed a technique to do it almost as quickly and simply as a vasectomy. This process is called a **laparoscopy.** A small incision is made in the navel (so that the scar will not be noticeable) and a miniature telescope is inserted, through which the doc-

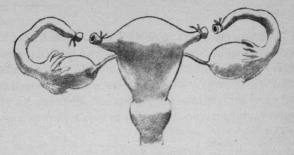

TUBAL LIGATION
(Sterilization of female)

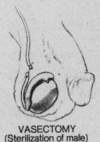

VASECTOMY
(Sterilization of male)

tor can see the fallopian tubes. The doctor also inserts an electric cauterizer to burn out a small section of each tube and to close up the ends so that no eggs or sperm can pass.

Neither a vasectomy nor a tubal ligation interferes with the enjoyment of sexual intercourse; they may actually increase enjoyment because the worry about pregnancy and the need for using any kind of device is gone. Both operations should be considered permanent, although another operation may be performed to undo them. But this second operation has much less than a fifty-fifty chance of succeeding and thus cannot be relied upon.

Abstinence

Abstinence means to abstain from—that is, not to have—sexual intercourse. However, since sexual sharing is such an important part of a couple's relationship and one of the ways that a couple have pleasure together and express their love for each other, abstinence is an unsatisfactory method of family planning.

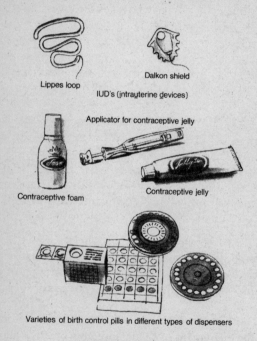

Lippes loop

Dalkon shield

IUD's (intrauterine devices)

Applicator for contraceptive jelly

Contraceptive foam

Contraceptive jelly

Varieties of birth control pills in different types of dispensers

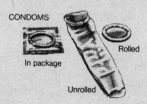

CONDOMS

In package

Rolled

Unrolled

The "Morning-after" Pill or Shot

If a woman has intercourse unexpectedly without using any reliable means of contraception, there is one last possibility for avoiding pregnancy. It is called the **"morning-after" pill** or **shot** and involves some massive doses of hormones. It is thought that these doses prevent implantation of the fertilized egg in the uterus. The doses usually make the woman who takes them very nauseated for a few days, and many doctors don't like to prescribe them. However, they cause no permanent harm, as far as is known.

Other methods of birth control are being investigated by scientisits and doctors, who feel, almost without exception, that necessary to mankind is a low-cost, easy, sure, safe method of limiting the size of families—and a method that will be acceptable to all.

It is important to emphasize that **there is much wrong and dangerous information passed around about birth control methods.** Some uninformed people try methods that **do not work,** like douches (squirting liquid into the vagina), Saran wrap, or urination right after intercourse. These methods do not work. The only way for a couple to be certain about a birth control method is to know that it is **medically approved** by the medical profession and that the product used is approved for birth control by the United States Food and Drug Administration.

Fortunately, it is now possible in most cities and in many rural areas for people to receive expert advice on contraception and to obtain the birth control products they need. Organizations like Planned Parenthood and most public health and medical centers provide these services, at no cost if the user cannot pay. No one should be afraid or embarrassed to ask for information about birth control. For any person who is going to have sex and is not ready to have and care for a child, it is a must.

It is interesting that many married couples have used the best methods of contraception with what they intended to be the greatest care, only to find that the wife has become pregnant and that a child is on the way. In rare cases, even vasectomies and tubal ligations may fail. By processes not entirely understood, the cut ends of the vas deferens or the fallopian tubes may reopen and reunite. However, failures of contraception are usually not failures of good methods but failures on the part of the people using them. Birth control can be counted upon to succeed only when used correctly and without haste.

Quite a lot of research has been done, on how reliable the different methods of contraception are, but researchers disagree, and, of course, **a great deal depends on how intelligently and conscientiously the couple use the method selected.** Out of any 100 women having intercourse regularly over a period of a year, how many will become pregnant during that year? Here are the best figures I can get:

Using no contraceptive at all	80—90 would be pregnant
Using withdrawal	30—40 would be pregnant
Using rhythm	15—35 would be pregnant
Using a recommended foam according to instructions	25 would be pregnant
Using condom	5—15 would be pregnant
Using diaphragm with sperm-killing cream or jelly	5—15 would be pregnant
Using IUD	3 would be pregnant

| Using pill | ½ (one in 200) would be pregnant |
| Being sterilized | almost none would be pregnant |

When properly used, then, methods of birth control do provide a satisfactory way of having sex without babies, of limiting the size of families, and of controlling the growth of the world's population.

Abortion——When Contraception Fails

If contraception fails, or a couple fail to use it, and the woman becomes pregnant, she will have to decide what to do. In Chapter 15, "Sex and Social Life," (pages 88–104), some of the possibilities are discussed. One of them is **abortion**—that is, to have the embryo removed by a simple surgical procedure before it has developed far enough to live. Today, when done early in pregnancy by a qualified physician in a hospital or specially equipped abortion clinic, abortions are relatively safe. However, no abortion is a minor matter, and abortions later in pregnancy present greater chance of surgical complications and often involve an overnight stay in the hospital. If the abortion is performed before the twelfth week of pregnancy, the doctor may use a recently developed suction machine which removes the embryo and other products of conception.

Obviously, the sooner a girl or woman reports an overdue menstrual period to her doctor or to a clinic, the better are the chances for less complicated and less expensive care.

When abortions are done in secret or illegally, it is almost impossible to check on the qualifications of the doctor or the adequacy of the equipment and procedures. In such cases, abortions may be dangerous and can permanently injure or even kill a woman.

Until recently, most states have had laws which did not allow doctors to perform abortions unless they were judged necessary to save the life and, in some states, to preserve the mental health of the mother. However, in 1973, the U.S. Supreme Court ruled that it is the right of any woman, in consultation with her doctor, to have an abortion performed within the first three months of pregnancy and that state laws interfering with this right are unconstitutional. After the first three months, states are allowed to pass laws regulating abortions in ways that are related to protecting the life or health of the mother. During the last three months of pregnancy, when the fetus may be **viable** (that is, if it is born prematurely and given proper special care, it could live), states are allowed to pass laws taking into consideration the welfare of the fetus as well as that of the mother.

There are many people, however, who feel that it is wrong to terminate even the beginnings of human life. They feel so strongly about this that they even say that abortion is murder, but most people feel that there is a very great difference between removing the products of conception that are growing toward a person, and murder, which involves the killing of an existing person, born and actually living out in the world. The Supreme Court's ruling stated that the U.S. Constitution considers a being to be a person only after he or she is born and said that we don't know enough at present to "resolve the difficult question of when life begins."

In any case, when a girl or woman is considering an abortion, it is important that she receive help and advice from a trained and sympathetic counselor as to whether she should continue or terminate her pregnancy. Quite often, the decision, either way, may affect her emotionally more deeply than she expected it would, and she needs help in dealing with these effects. The counselor will also see that she gets contraceptive advice so that abortion, if that is her decision, will not be necessary again.

Abortion is certainly a very poor method of birth control, even though more and more people are coming to believe that it is better than allowing an unwanted child to be born into what may be for him or her a hostile world.

14

VD: The Diseases of Sex

Another problem of sex is **venereal disease.** (The word "venereal" means "having to do with sexual intercourse" and comes from the name Venus, the Roman goddess of love.) Sexual intercourse itself doesn't cause VD, but engaging in sexual intercourse or heavy petting with an infected person may give it to you. In the late 1960s, after a long period of decline, VD began to increase rapidly in the United States, especially among teen-agers, and it is very important for everyone who is sexually active to know about it. There are two main venereal diseases, **gonorrhea** and **syphilis.**

Gonorrhea

Commonly called "the clap," "the drip," or "a dose," gonorrhea seldom causes death, but if not treated promptly it can often cause sterility and crippling arthritis. The disease is caused by the gonococcus germ, which can live only in warm, moist places, such as inside the human body, and it usually gets its start inside the vagina or the penis and the rest of the reproduction tract. Gonorrhea is epidemic throughout the world today, being the most common serious infectious disease in the United States.

It is easy for a man to know he has gonorrhea, because a few days after he has become infected he will notice a painful burning when he urinates and pus will drip from his penis. Without having a special test, it is often impossible for a woman to know she has gonorrhea. She may have no easily noticeable symptoms at all, since the gonococcus germs usually live and multiply around her cervix, where the tissue is less delicate than that in the urethra and where no urine, with its acid content, passes over the area. The gonococci usually do not spread to the woman's urethra (see diagram, p. 5). Thus, if a man knows he has contracted gonorrhea, he should at once tell any woman with whom he has had sexual intercourse, so that she may be examined at once and treated if need be. If she is infected and not treated, the disease will damage her body, and she may transmit it to other sexual partners.

The treatment is simple: usually a few shots of penicillin. This will nearly always cure a person but it will **not** prevent him or her from getting the disease again. There is no immunity.

If gonorrhea is not treated, the germs often spread throughout the body, damaging the sex organs and the joints. When the body attempts to repair the damage, it may cause scar tissue to block the sperm tubes and tubules in a man, or the fallopian tubes in a woman, preventing the sperm or the egg from getting through. In this way, gonorrhea is a major cause of **sterility**—the inability to have children—in men and women.

Gonorrhea can also damage the eyes and used to be a major cause of blindness in babies born to mothers who were infected at the time. Now the law requires that special drops or medicated jelly be put in the eyes of a newborn baby, and this has made gonorrheal blindness quite rare in this country.

Syphilis

Syphilis is caused by little corkscrewlike organisms called **spirochetes** which circulate in the bloodstream and burrow deep into the tissues of the body, where they may lie inactive for years. This disease kills hundreds, perhaps thousands, of men and women each year, and also causes blindness, heart disease, insanity, and many other ailments. It appears in many forms and stages and can cause most painful suffering. Also, it can be passed on to an unborn child through a mother who has not been adequately treated.

Fortunately, as soon as it is discovered the disease can be treated quite easily with large doses of penicillin or other antibiotics. Also, there are reliable blood tests for it, which most states require of a man and a woman before they are permitted to marry. This is not to say that syphilis is no longer a grave problem. It is. For one thing, a person cannot easily recognize syphilis in its early stages because its first symptoms are usually slight or similar to those of several other diseases. The most common symptom is a hard, painless, moist sore called a **chancre.** It usually appears, from ten days to three months after exposure, at the place where the spirochetes entered the body, in the man usually on the penis and in the woman deep within the vagina, where it cannot be seen. After a short time, from a few days to a month, the chancre disappears without any treatment, but this does **not** mean the syphilis has disappeared. It has merely gone "underground." Later it may cause other symptoms: a nonitching rash most often on the palms or soles, or hair falling out in patches, plus a sore throat, low fever, and aching, somewhat like the symptoms of the "flu." But these symptoms also disappear, and then the spirochetes spread undetected throughout the body, where, over the years, they may damage the organs and cause serious diseases and, not infrequently, death. Many people die of syphilis damage without ever knowing the real cause of their sickness.

Most cases of syphilis and gonorrhea are transmitted by sexual intercourse. However, it is possible, in rare cases, for a young girl to get gonorrhea from a warm, moist towel just used by someone who has it, and syphilis can be spread by "deep kissing" a person who has a chancre or syphilitic mucous patches in his or her mouth. Both diseases can be passed during heavy petting with an infected person. In very rare cases, doctors have been infected with syphilis through a scratch or cut while they were handling a syphilitic baby.

If you remember that venereal disease germs can stay alive only for a few minutes unless they remain moist and at body temperature, you will see how nearly impossible it is to catch VD from such things as a toilet seat or doorknob. Almost always, it is contracted from close sexual contact with a person who has it.

If a couple have been examined by a doctor to make sure that neither one is infected (and this necessitates a blood test for syphilis and a culture for gonorrhea), and if thereafter they have sex only with each other, they need not worry about VD. The people most likely to get VD are those who are sexually **promiscuous**—that is, who are sexually active with a variety of partners. If someone you do not know well is willing to have sex with you, quite likely that person has had sex with other people, too, and your chances of getting VD are pretty high. You should remember that it is almost impossible to tell by a person's appearance whether he or she has VD, and if the person is selfish or not caring, he or she may not tell you about an infection.

One encouraging thing about VD is that it is quite easily treated and cured. Therefore, if you have any reason to believe you have been exposed to VD infection, you should go **at once** to a public health clinic or to your own doctor for tests. You should be sure to tell the doctor that you think you may have been exposed to VD and ask for tests for **both** syphilis and gonorrhea. If you do not ask, the doctor will probably not do the necessary tests. You need not feel embarrassed, for such tests and any needed treatment are kept confidential. If you have a venereal disease, it is important, too, that the person with whom you have had sexual contact also be tested and treated.

If you need help in finding a public health clinic near you where you can be tested and, if necessary, treated without cost, or if you have questions about VD, you may call Operation Venus. This is an organization primarily of concerned teen-agers, assisted by VD experts, which maintains a free VD "hot line." Call them free of charge between 9 A.M. and 9 P.M. at one of these numbers:

800-523-1885 (anywhere in the USA except Pennsylvania).

215-567-6973 (in Pennsylvania, outside of Philadelphia area. You may call collect).

567-6969 (in the Philadelphia area).

Your call is kept confidential. No one asks for your name.

Another encouraging thing about VD is that syphilis could be wiped out as a health problem in our nation as completely as polio and smallpox and typhoid have been; and gonorrhea could at least be brought under control. This was shown during World War II. After VD had become a major health problem among American troops, the armed forces supplied condoms (which, if used properly, before any genital contact, give fair protection against the spread of VD) and penicillin quite freely to the men, and VD was almost eliminated among them. If enough money were made available, if the dangers of VD and the ease of treatment were publicized, if laws were passed requiring testing and treatment, and if more anti-VD workers were trained and set to work, in a short time we could be free of the discomfort, danger, damage, and vast expense of VD, and at a very small cost compared to the costs of allowing VD to spread relatively out of control, as it is now. We know what needs to be done; all we need is the national will to do it.

There are several other diseases and discomforts from which women having sexual intercourse sometimes suffer. There are so-called **yeast infections,** and other vaginal infections, which cause itching and burning. There are also **urinary infections,** which arise because the woman's opening for urine is right next to the vagina and therefore subject to infection. These may cause painful urination or kidney pain (backache).

Both men and women may be afflicted with **crabs,** a kind of lice which get into the pubic hair and cause itching. If you think you may be infected with any of these diseases, or have any unusual symptoms in your genital area, see a doctor or go to a clinic at once for testing and any needed treatment.

15

Sex and Social Life

Human beings have been called "social animals." They relate to each other in thousands of different ways, some ways that are loving and caring, some that are hateful and selfish. They can help each other and enrich life for each other, or they can exploit—use—each other and put each other down.

A part of being a social animal is **communication.** Some people are much better at it than others, and probably all of us could learn to communicate more easily and fully than we do. One of the ways we share our thoughts and feelings is with our bodies: through our facial expressions, our gestures, our ways of sitting, standing, and moving, through the ways we touch or do not touch each other. We also communicate through words, by what we say to each other and how we say it. Unlike other animals, whose ways of communication are programmed into them by instinct, we human beings **learn** to communicate. We start learning almost as soon as we are born, and we go right on learning throughout our lives. Certainly, in those parts of our lives which involve sex and sexual feelings, communication is most important, but for many people, most difficult. There are many married couples who have lived together for years and yet have hardly ever talked with each other directly and openly about sex and about their sexual feelings toward each other.

There is no way to separate sexual life from the

other parts of life, although some people try to make such a separation. Indeed, this book, which talks mainly about sex, may seem to make such a separation. But sex and sexuality are a part of life, a part to accept and live with, to enjoy. Sex is not something from outside that comes in, takes over our bodies temporarily, and then flies off. Some people, however, do see sex in the separate way, and they may use this as an explanation, or even an excuse, for sexual actions that are damaging. "I really didn't want intercourse; the feelings just came and overwhelmed me." True, it is possible to be overwhelmed by sexual feelings, but these feelings are a part of our other feelings.

It is also possible to deny our sexual feelings, as if they were something bad and apart that should be pushed away or pushed under. We must learn to **integrate** our sexual feelings and actions with all the rest of our living.

One fact that enriches our social lives is that there are two sexes, male and female. In Chapter 9 you read about differences between men and women, how some of them are inborn and inevitable, but how in many ways we learn to be "masculine" and "feminine," and how in modern life it has become possible for us to be much more free to develop into the sort of people we want to be, not so limited by traditional sex roles. We can enjoy relating to each other as women and as men, and also, even more important, as human beings who share so much in common. The sexual part of a relationship, whether it involves sexual activity or whether it involves only the expression of our human sexuality, can add a delight and pleasure that would be absent if there were only one sex. Differences—those based on sex and those based on age, background, interests, personality, work, language, culture, nationality, and thousand other things—can be just as important to good, rich relationships as can similarities.

Sex cannot be separated from the rest of life, but there are special things to be said about the pleasures and problems of love and sex as part of life. One of the problems of sex that human beings have and animals don't have can be stated quite simply: boys and girls reach puberty (when so many of them begin to have strong sexual desires) before they are old enough to enter into a full and satisfying sexual relationship, to marry, or to establish a family and raise children. There is a period of from eight to ten years or even longer when the sex urge is strong but there is no way to satisfy it that is entirely acceptable to all parts of our society.

Some boys and girls, concerned that they might not be able to have a good sex life later on if they do not use their sex organs for a number of years, ask if these organs dry up or grow weak with disuse, just as muscles grow weak if they are not exercised. The answer is "No." Sex organs and muscles are quite different. It is true that there are some people who, when they marry, have difficulty in learning to enjoy sex freely after they have developed the habit, ever since puberty, of turning themselves off sexually every time they felt aroused, but most people who have no intercourse until they marry find that their sexual power is strong and adequate.

In thinking and talking about sexual activity during adolescence, it is important to remember that **adolescence is a process of growing toward maturity.** The decisions that boys and girls make will differ with different people, with the strength of their sex drive, the beliefs and teaching they have been exposed to and how they reacted to them, the social situations they are in, and values and convictions they develop. Few people ever find final answers for questions as complicated as those relating to sexual behavior. Most of us will go on searching and questioning during all of our lives. And it is most likely that we are not going to be willing to behave in certain ways just because we are **told** to. Most of us will put together the information we have, the values we hold, our idea of the sort of person we want to be, and the things we have been told—and then decide for ourselves. If we are responsible, mature people, our decisions will be made in the light of knowledge of all of the consequences of what we do, consequences good and bad, present and future, for us and for others.

If the consequences of the actions are likely to be good for all the people involved—for self, partner, family, community, nation, world—both now and in the future, then perhaps we can say that the actions are **moral.** If they are bad, and especially if the person performing the actions knows they may be bad and does them anyway, then they are **immoral.** You can see that there is nothing easy about these definitions of "moral" and "immoral." That is why it is such a good idea to talk over your questions about sexual behavior, and all other important kinds of behavior, with people your own age and also with those who have had more life experience than you have and whose wisdom and judgment you respect.

One thing is sure: people's degree of sexual readiness changes as they grow toward maturity. Twelve- to fourteen-year-olds are vastly different from, say, seventeen- to nineteen-year-olds. And, of course, the degree of readiness depends on the individual person and his or her interests, circumstances, values, and maturity.

Another thing is sure, too: some junior-high-schoolers are already having sexual intercourse, whether their parents, their schools, or society approve or not. On the other hand, many people who have reached adulthood are not having and never have had sexual intercourse.

As for how much sex it is right to have at what age, there are probably nearly as many opinions as there are thinking people. Here are two opinions, expressed in class by eighth-graders whom I have taught, which show the differences there can be even among people the same age. Both were spoken by boys, but I think they could just as well have been said by girls. I write them down to the best of my memory, although I am sure I haven't succeeded in using the exact words of each speaker.

One said: "I think sex is recreation, and it should be enjoyed just like any other recreation. Sex gives big physical pleasure and can help two people communicate deeply with each other. If a girl and a boy know what they are doing—I mean, if they take proper precautions to avoid having a baby, and if they are alert to the dangers of VD—then why shouldn't they have sex?

"I don't think they even have to be in love. As long as they both want to do it, they should go ahead and have sex pleasure. It's natural. After all, girls and boys talk together, they dance together, they play together, and all sorts of things like that. Why shouldn't they have sexual intercourse together?"

The other said: "I think the basis for our society is families. And the center of the family is a married couple who ought to love each other. The couple make a home based on their relationship, and this home brings love and security to them and their children.

"A great part of the husband and wife's relationship is sex—not all, but a big part. Having sex helps to keep them close and loyal to each other. There's something absolutely special about having sex, I think, even though I haven't had it yet. I'm not going to have it until I get married, and then I'm only going to have it with my wife.

"I'm not saying that you shouldn't make out some before you're married. That's O.K. if you like each other and it would help you get to know each other. But sexual intercourse—that should be saved for marriage."

These two students express two contrasting points of view very well, I think. You may agree with one or the other, or partly with each, and your views will probably change as you mature and grow older.

Certainly, it is natural for boys and girls to be interested in each other and to be interested in sex. If boys and girls get to know each other well, they can learn to understand and appreciate their differences and likenesses, and this is excellent preparation for the future and for choosing a husband or wife if they decide they want to marry. When you think about marriage, it's important to remember that you will marry not primarily a body, but a **person**—a complex human being with a background of life experience different from yours. The person's body will be important, but not nearly so important in the long run as his or her personality and character.

There is certainly no point in hurrying boy-girl relationships along faster than you desire. Most people in their early teens are not yet ready for an intense relationship with a member of the opposite sex. As a matter of fact, a good many boys between the ages of ten and thirteen or even older find girls most **un**desirable, even if they are very curious about them. And many girls in the same age group find their boy classmates to be loud, awkward, childish, and generally repulsive. That's all right; it is likely to change in a few years.

However, it is a good idea for boys and girls to have ample opportunities to get to know each other socially, if they want to. There is a lot of room for friendships between boys and girls in their early teens (but little reason for concern if such friendship doesn't develop).

There is much pleasure to be had from informal parties, dances, picnics, and other group get-togethers, with enough activities planned in advance, and with parents helping, and also from hiking, bicycle, and camping trips.

It is a rare seventh- or eighth-grader who is ready to go steady. A boy and girl who do so at this age may have a pretty dreary and limited life after the first excitement of it. The teens is a good period of life for getting to know many people of both sexes and to know them in many different ways.

In typical classes of twelve- to fourteen-year-olds there are usually a few boys and girls who get all steamed up about parties and dances, about cliques, about who is

most popular, and who likes whom. They—especially the girls—seem to be afraid that if they don't start being popular right away and don't become big wheels socially as soon as possible, or in with the most-In group, they may never have a chance. There is no question that their fears are real, but they are not based on fact. I've known many, many boys and girls who were miserable because they weren't making it socially in junior high school who in later grades or in college became popular and enjoyed real social success. Perhaps the true measure of success is not the number of friendships one has but the quality of those friendships.

Many young teen-agers can even benefit from learning what it is like to be hurt by not enjoying immediate popularity, by having to work to **achieve** social success. Such experience can teach boys and girls to understand the feelings of others, to be considerate of them, and to do their best to please them. In this way they learn that a lasting relationship between people has to be built on more than physical attractiveness and a good line of conversation. The most important parts of the relationship are common interests and mutual consideration.

In my experience in schools, I have often been saddened, and sometimes angered, by the cruel way that some boys and girls, more often boys, ridicule classmates whom they consider different from themselves. Often this ridicule, which includes name-calling, is directed against boys whose physical development is slower than that of most of their classmates or who are not particularly interested in sports, vigorous physical activity, and the sorts of behavior that we too easily label as "male." It is wrong, both factually and morally, to take part in such cruel activities, even though they may not be intended to be cruel. It is wrong factually because it assumes that any boy or girl who is not "all boy" or "all girl" is probably going to turn out to be a homosexual, which simply is not so. We usually cannot tell who is going to turn out to be gay and who straight. It is wrong morally because it is cruel, puts people down, and makes them feel bad about themselves. Also, it assumes that there is only one right way to turn out.

It is not easy for most of us to be considerate of the feelings, preferences, and personalities of other people all of the time, especially of people we see as different from ourselves, but it is a sign of maturity to show such consideration.

I want to say a few words about **necking** and **petting,** which you probably have discussed, wondered about, and possibly experimented with. Necking is generally understood to include putting your arms around a person's neck or waist, holding hands, sitting close or cheek to cheek, and light kissing. It is a way of expressing your affection for that person, but it does not involve trying to arouse him or her to readiness for sexual intercourse. Petting goes much further and involves caressing the most sensitive parts of the body, such as the breasts or genitals, and deep kissing. It is the kind of lovemaking that makes a couple ready for intercourse. The term **making out** can refer to either necking or petting.

It's only natural and healthy to feel like expressing your affection for other people by touching them. It is a delightful fact that babies and little children crave and need lots of physical love from their parents or those who care for them, and you have probably many times in the past enjoyed a good hug and kiss from your mother or father—and other relatives, too. There can be a similar sort of enjoyment and warmth in physical contact with a member of the other sex who is near your age. Even so, there are some very important things to be kept in mind concerning such physical contact, particularly by boys and girls in their teens:

● Kissing and caressing can not only bring great pleasure, closeness, and good feelings; they may also lead to difficulty. Some boys quickly become so aroused sexually that they lose their willingness to control themselves, and a girl may have difficulty in controlling them. It is also just as possible for some girls to become so involved that they, too, lose the will to stop, expecially if earlier experiences have taught them how pleasurable sexual feeling is. In other words, if you have not decided for yourself, and **in advance** of a petting experience, where you are going to stop, or even whether you are going to start, you may find yourself involved in situations where your physical feelings overwhelm you. You may find yourself engaging in sexual intercourse when you would not have chosen to if you had thought about it. When that happens, and you are unprepared, both emotionally and with contraceptives, the long-term results may be tragic.

Of course, the situation may be quite different if both partners are physically and emotionally mature enough to manage the powerful feelings and effects of intercourse, if both intend and want to have sex, and both are prepared for it—that is, have communicated with each other long enough and deeply enough so that they understand and consider each other's feelings, and have agreed upon using an effective means of contraception.

Each partner needs to be aware of the possibility that some boys and girls may try to "use" a partner of the other sex—or sometimes the same sex—in order to satisfy only their own needs—needs to feel important, to feel that they have made it or "scored," that they are keeping up with their friends or competitors, that they will have something to boast about. People whose feelings of insecurity give them a lot of trouble, or who are extremely selfish, may become very persuasive in trying to argue a partner into having sexual intercourse. They may pretend to be in love, or even persuade themselves that they are in love; they may threaten to cut off a relationship unless their partner will "go all the way" with them; they may try to make their partner feel small or immature or afraid of not going along; or they may say, in effect, "if you love me, you will prove it by having sex with me."

● A fact to remember about heavy petting is that it is possible—although such a happening is rather rare—for a girl to become pregnant even though she has an intact hymen and has never had intercourse. There is the natural opening in the hymen through which menstruation flows. If, in the course of heavy petting, the boy ejaculates near this opening, sperm may make their way into the vagina even though actual intercourse has not taken place. It is because sperm are such active swimmers that they may cause a pregnancy in a girl who is technically still a virgin.

● As I have said, there comes an age and a degree of maturity and experience, certainly not the same age for all, when some adolescents feel they are ready for heavy petting and when they start thinking and talking about whether or not to have sexual intercourse. Here, while I am discussing petting, I want to add a word about the strong desire that most adolescent boys, and many girls, feel to experience the full sexual satisfaction of an orgasm. For unmarried people, especially young and immature ones, probably intercourse is not the best way to do this, all things considered. In Chapter 11, I discussed masturbation as a harmless way of achieving orgasm. There are some couples who masturbate together. If a boy and a girl do engage in this sort of petting to orgasm, it is very important that they be considerate of each other, and especially that the boy understand that his partner may be feeling much less sexually aroused than he—possibly not aroused at all. The girl, on the other hand, should know that what she may have meant to be only a friendly touch may be taken quite differently by the boy—as an invitation to go much further than she wants to go.

These differences help explain why knowing how to talk about sexual feelings with one's partner is so important to a happy, healthy, and satisfying sexual life.

● Boys and girls should not feel pushed into necking and petting, or into intercourse, by their friends or the customs of their group. There are many teen-age boys and girls who do not want to engage in physical expressions of affection or who are quite embarrassed by them. They may want to wait until they have grown up more; they may have other, keener interests; they may not yet feel ready for the emotional effects. Certainly, you should not allow yourself to be pressured into sexual activity you do not want just because you are afraid that people will think you are square or not "with it" unless you are sexually active. Many young people feel deeply, like the second boy I quoted on page 92, that they want to save the intense physical expressions of love until they are married, when they can expect to have a lifetime of loving and caring, and of learning together the ways that a couple can give and receive sexual satisfaction.

● Another consideration to keep in mind is that many people, especially older people, have been brought up to feel, and still feel deeply, that expressions of affection between boys and girls should be inconspicuous—not public. They consider this simply a matter of good taste. Boys and girls who go against the standards that many people feel are acceptable are likely to make such people unhappy or uncomfortable, and are likely to be criticized.

I have spoken of some of the pleasures and rewards of the sexual side of human social life—and of some cares and cautions that you should exercise. Perhaps, though, you may be thinking, like the first eighth-grader quoted on page 92, "Well, when you are old enough to feel like satisfying your sexual drive, why not just find a member of the other sex who is willing and go ahead and satisfy it?" Before you decide on this, here are some more important considerations to think through:

● Sexual intercourse, as I have suggested, is for most people a deeply moving experience, not something to be played around with casually. It almost always involves not only the body but also the mind and the emotions—one's deepest feelings. It also involves nature's means for carrying on the human race. These facts explain why, when a couple have intercourse as an expression of their love for each other and commitment to each other, it can bring them even closer together.

But when two people do not care about each other, they may feel guilty or ashamed after having intercourse. This is especially true of girls. When sexual intercourse is undertaken too lightly, it goes against the customs and moral feelings developed through many generations of our culture. If these feelings are deeply engrained in people as a part of their upbringing, **premarital intercourse** (intercourse before marriage) may result in their not feeling quite right about themselves, and it may make it more difficult for them, later on, to take part in a good, happy sexual relationship.

However, there are no reliable statistics that show that people who have premarital intercourse are more or less likely to have successful and happy marriages than those who do not. True, there are many people who make quite confident statements on this matter—either for or against premarital intercourse—but their statements are more matters of personal belief or of what they think **ought** to be the case than of what can be **shown** to be the case, based on facts.

● The major religions in the United States teach that it is morally wrong to have sexual intercourse outside of marriage, although in recent years many churches have relaxed their teaching about this, expecially about premarital intercourse. Fortunately, today many churches provide sex and family-life education to help young people deal responsibly with their sexuality.

However, if people's religions do teach that premarital intercourse is wrong and they disregard the teaching, they may feel guilty, and this feeling may isolate them from a source of strength, comfort, and confidence that would help them.

● Young unmarried people who have sexual intercourse take a risk: the couple may have a child, which will very likely be a tragedy for both of them and for the baby, because the parents are rarely mature enough to marry and establish a family. Neither one is ready to earn a living to support a family; both the boy and the girl probably should have years of education ahead of them, which marriage may interrupt. If they had waited, they would have been wiser, more stable, and more experienced in life—better prepared to choose a marriage partner and to manage family life. Therefore, if an unmarried couple is going to engage in intercourse, they should do so only after thinking about it and exploring their feelings with great care. It would be best if they were able to find some older and understanding person with whom they could talk confidentially without fear of being disapproved of or condemned. Such a person could help them think through all the pros and cons. Certainly, if they decide to have sex, they should make careful plans for contraception (see Chapter 14) and not just "take a chance" by allowing themselves to be swept into it by the emotions of the moment, which may be quite different from the emotions of loving and caring.

● A young unmarried couple who produce a child they do not want and are not prepared to care for may feel forced into marriage by family or church. They will have to marry in haste and probably not because they have chosen each other as life partners. Their chances of married happiness are small, experience shows. Before long the boy and girl may feel angry at each other for all of the difficulty that has been caused. What may have started off as a happy moment has resulted in a heavy burden that may never be entirely unloaded. The divorce rate among such young couples is unusually high—at least one out of every two marriages within five years. Divorce usually leaves a baby and its mother to struggle alone; and a young father is left with the legal obligation, unless his former wife marries again, to support them in addition to the second wife and the family he may eventually have.

If the couple do not marry, the girl often is left without a partner to share the responsibilities of parenthood. Perhaps with the help of her own family, she will have the child and give it adequate care. Perhaps she will place it for adoption. Whatever she does, she is likely to think of it with deep concern all of her life.

Some girls, when they become pregnant, seek an abortion. This you have read about, pages 79–81.

● One other possible consequence of sexual intercourse, especially casual intercourse with several partners, is venereal disease. Today, VD is easily cured, but it is also widespread and is causing serious discomfort and damage. You have read about this problem in Chapter 14.

Boys and girls often ask about the effects of alcohol and drugs on sexual feelings and performance. Alcohol does have the effect of reducing a person's self-control and inhibitions. A famous cartoon by George Price shows an eager-looking man at a bar standing behind a sexy-looking young woman and saying to the bartender, "Fill her up!"

Even moderate amount of alcohol tends to relax people's inhibitions, to make them less likely to say no. However, self-control, especially when a couple is not married and not well-prepared or mature, is what both urgently need in a sexual situation. Aside from the lessening of self-control, alcohol, especially if quite a lot is taken, has a depressing effect on a boy's ability to have an erection and to ejaculate and on a girl's ability either to respond to or to reject sexual relations.

As for drugs, the situation is complicated. Marijuana may, like alcohol, relax a person. Some users say that it heightens sexual feelings. It also lessens self-control and may sometimes reduce the ability to have an orgasm. Stimulant drugs, such as "speed," reduce the ability to perform sexually. "Heavy" drugs like heroin knock a person out sexually, although they don't knock out his imagination.

If you feel that you need the crutch of alcohol or drugs to make sex acceptable or good, you have a problem, and alcohol or drugs won't solve it. What you need is to talk to a counselor and get some help before taking the risks that sex involves. Alcohol and drugs can make you less able to deal intelligently with sexual feelings.

This chapter has placed more emphasis on the problems and possibly unhappy consequences of sexual activity entered into thoughtlessly and irresponsibly, without communication and preparation, than on the pleasure and deep satisfactions growing from sexual relationships based on consideration, caring, and love. This is because I am convinced that to manage the responsibilities of your life you need to know both the bad news and the good news about sex and social life. The bad news may take more time to tell, but the good news is certainly more important.

16

Some Values to Guide You

If you are like most people, your whole life, including your sex life and your experiences with love, will have its ups and downs, its great joys, and its sorrows and regrets. Much depends on how you take what life brings to you and the values by which you make your decisions. I am talking about both your life now, in adolescence, and about your life later as an adult, whether or not you marry.

And, by the way, I hope you will not let yourself be hurried into marriage too soon. There are many people who benefit by waiting to get married; and there are many who probably should never marry at all, or who have never found a person as pleasing to them as the rewards of living singly or in a group. An attractive, loving, lovable, older Quaker lady, a member of my Friends meeting, smilingly said to a friend when she was asked why she had never married: "Well, thee knows, it takes a mighty good husband to be better than none."

We all know also of unmarried people who live full, satisfying lives because they have found that the deep and rewarding demands of a career are more important than the satisfactions of marriage, which might prevent the fullest accomplishment in a career.

Questions about career, marriage, and having or not having children, about the conduct of your sex life, are questions you will be deciding for yourself. All through your life, but especially during your adolescence, you will be searching for your own set of values to guide you, and one of the signs of being mature is to have developed a sound set of values, even though the search for values should never stop. I want to end this book by suggesting six values which may help to guide you as you make decisions about love and sex and life. Some of them, as you will see, I've already spoken about, but they bear re-emphasizing here.

The first is the value of **information.** Correct information—the facts—is better than ignorance or rumor. Sound information makes it possible for you to act responsibly. Ignorance may get you into trouble

The second value is **responsibility.** If you are a responsible person, you undertake the actions of your life **keeping in mind what the results, the consequences, of your action will be**—the consequences for yourself and for all the others involved, both now and in the future.

The third value is **control.** Sex is a power. Like any other power, it can be used for good or for bad. We all need to learn to control our sexual power so that we use it for good—of ourselves and others. (Two other examples of power where control makes all the difference between benefit and tragedy are fire and the automobile.)

The fourth value is **consideration.** We should do what we do while considering and caring for our own needs, feelings, and welfare, and for those of others. To be truly considerate of others we need to have enough thoughtfulness and imagination to put ourselves in their shoes—in their skin, as some say.

The fifth value is the **worth of each individual person.** To understand this infinite worth and to respect it, we need to feel our own worth. Self-respect is the beginning of respect for others and for their worth.

The sixth value is that of **communication.** It is good to be able to talk things over with other people. It is good for boys and girls and men and women to be able to talk with each other about their sexual feelings, desires, and fears. I hope this book will help you to do this with your friends and with your parents. Sometimes, if you have all read the same book, the way to communication is more easily opened.

And so, a last word about love and sex. Remember that love is a complicated relationship, and that sexual love is only one part of it. There are other loves: the unreserved support and loyalty found between many parents and their children; the ease comfortableness and enjoyment that come from the love of a friend; the zest and stimulation that are a kind of love felt by people who share common tasks, interests, and problems. I know a young married couple who are happy and satisfied together. The wife, who is author of an excellent short book called *Practical Sex Information* (published by Waking Woman Press) expressed the "most important aspect" of their marriage thus: "We are very-best-friends; we enjoy each other's company more entirely than anyone else's; we have each other to come home to and tell our adventures in the big world. We are pretty sure that without this aspect we would have nothing, and that there is nothing else more important in our relationship."

When two people have great affection for each other and understand each other well, and when they make a commitment to join their lives and to care for each other through thick and thin, then the sexual part of their love, each for the other, can grow ever more satisfying, joyful, and deep.

Index

ABOUT THE AUTHOR

ERIC W. JOHNSON teaches English and is involved in the sex education program at Philadelphia's Germantown Friends School. Mr. Johnson has served overseas with the American Friends Service Committee in Portugal, Morocco, Algeria, India, France and Russia. He speaks frequently on sex education to teachers, school administrators and parent groups. He is also the author of *Sex: Telling It Straight, How to Live Through Junior High School* and *V.D.*